Attitudes and Persuasion

'. . . students entering this field tend to be faced with a mass of theories and studies that are rather incomprehensible unless one has a 'map'. . . This short text provides such a map . . . the "light" writing style and use of everyday examples will surely ensure that it works as an attractive and easy to follow guide.'

Nick Hopkins,
University of Dundee

Attitudes and Persuasion provides an up-to-date overview of the crucial role that attitudes play in our everyday lives and how our thoughts and behaviour are influenced. The nature, function and origins of attitudes are examined, and a review of how they can be measured is given. The book addresses complex questions such as whether we always behave in accordance with our attitudes and what factors may persuade us to change them.

Phil Erwin has written an accessible account of this major branch of social psychology, appropriate for students on a wide variety of undergraduate courses who may be studying these issues for the first time.

Phil Erwin teaches psychology at Edge Hill College, Ormskirk. He has carried out research in social psychology for over 20 years and is the author of *Friendship in Childhood and Adolescence*, also in this series.

Psychology Focus

Series editor: Perry Hinton, University of Luton

The Psychology Focus series provides students with a new focus on key topic areas in psychology. It supports students taking modules in psychology, whether for a psychology degree or a combined programme, and those renewing their qualification in a related discipline. Each short book:

- presents clear, in-depth coverage of a discrete area with many applied examples
- assumes no prior knowledge of psychology
- has been written by an experienced teacher
- has chapter summaries, annotated further reading and a glossary of key terms.

Also available in this series:

Attitudes and Persuasion

- Phil Erwin

PSYCHOLOGY PRESS
ALERE FLAMMAM
Taylor & Francis Group

First published 2001
by Psychology Press Ltd
27 Church Road, Hove, East Sussex
BN3 2FA
www.psypress.co.uk

Simultaneously published in
the USA and Canada
by Taylor & Francis, Inc.
325 Chestnut Street, Suite 800,
Philadelphia, PA 19016

*Psychology Press is part of the Taylor
& Francis Group*

© 2001 Phil Erwin

Typeset in Sabon and Futura by
Florence Production Ltd, Stoodleigh,
Devon

Cover design by Terry Foley

Printed and bound in Great Britain by
TJ International Ltd, Padstow,
Cornwall

*British Library Cataloguing in
Publication Data*
A catalogue record for this book is
available from the British Library

*Library of Congress Cataloging-in-
Publication Data*
Erwin, Phil.
  Attitudes and persuasion/by Phil
Erwin
  p. cm. — (Psychology focus series)
Includes bibliographical references
and index.
ISBN 0–415–19621–3
ISBN 0–415–19622–1 (pbk.)
  1. Attitude (Psycholgy) 2. Attitude
change. 3. Persuasion (Psychology)
  I. Title. II. Psychology focus

BF327. E76 2001
152.4—dc21   2001019720

ISBN 0–415–19621–3 (hbk)

ISBN 0–415–19622–1 (pbk)

Contents

CONTENTS

Series preface

The Psychology Focus series provides short, up-to-date accounts of key areas in psychology without assuming the reader's prior knowledge in the subject. Psychology is often a favoured subject area for study, since it is relevant to a wide range of disciplines such as Sociology, Education, Nursing and Business Studies. These relatively inexpensive but focused short texts combine sufficient detail for psychology specialists with sufficient clarity for non-specialists.

The series authors are academics experienced in undergraduate teaching as well as research. Each takes a topic within their area of psychological expertise and presents a short review, highlighting important themes and including both theory and research findings. Each aspect of the topic is clearly explained with supporting glossaries to elucidate technical terms.

The series has been conceived within the context of the increasing modularisation which has been developed in higher education over the last decade and fulfils the consequent need for clear, focused, topic-based course material. Instead of following one course of study, students on a modularisation programme are often able to choose modules from a wide range of disciplines to complement the modules they are required to study for a specific degree. It can no longer be assumed that students studying a particular module will necessarily have the same background knowledge (or lack of it!) in that subject. But they will need to familiarise themselves with a particular topic rapidly since a single module in a single topic may be only 15 weeks long, with assessments arising during that period. They may have to combine eight or more modules in a single year to obtain a degree at the end of their programme of study.

One possible problem with studying a range of separate modules is that the relevance of a particular topic or the relationship between topics may not always be apparent. In the Psychology Focus series, authors have drawn where possible on practical and applied examples to support the points being made so that readers can see the wider relevance of the topic under study. Also, the study of psychology is usually broken up into separate areas, such as social psychology, developmental psychology and cognitive psychology, to take three examples. Whilst the books in the Psychology Focus series will provide excellent coverage of certain key topics within these 'traditional' areas, the authors have not been constrained in their examples and explanations and may draw on material across the whole field of psychology to help explain the topic under study more fully.

Each text in the series provides the reader with a range of important material on a specific topic. They are suitably comprehensive and give a clear account of the important issues involved. The authors analyse and interpret the material as well as present an up-to-date and detailed review of key work. Recent references are provided along with suggested further reading to allow readers to investigate the topic in more depth. It is hoped, therefore, that after following the informative review of a key topic in a Psychology Focus text, readers not only will have a clear understanding of the issues in question but will be intrigued and challenged to investigate the topic further.

Chapter 1

Attitudes: definitions and theories

1

Introduction

A TTITUDES ARE CRUCIAL TO our everyday lives. They help us to interpret our surroundings, guide our behaviour in social situations and organise our experiences into a personally meaningful whole. Without attitudes the world would be a much less predictable place and we would function in it much less effectively. As an example, it would be impossible to establish and maintain any sort of relationship with another person without the involvement of attitudes. What you think of other people, the characteristics that are important to you and how you evaluate them, are components in an interpersonal attitude. Similarly, your attitudes will influence how you act on the beliefs and evaluations you hold about other people. If the other person is a stranger, is it appropriate for you to approach them and speak to them, or should you respect their privacy? This will also be affected by how you interpret the current situation in which you find yourself. If the other person is someone you know, your attitudes will guide you on how to manage social interaction with them. They will determine topics you regard as appropriate to disclose and discuss with the person, how you expect them to behave in the relationship, and how you feel about them. In this book I will introduce some of the major ideas about the nature and structure of attitudes, their significance for personal adjust-

2

ment and functioning, and the ways in which they may change or be changed.

Thomas and Znaniecki (1918) are often credited with writing the paper that first brought attitudes to a place of central prominence within social psychology. They saw attitudes as 'determining what an individual sees, hears, thinks and, supposedly, does'. They even went so far as to define social psychology as 'the science of attitudes'! Perhaps a little less ambitiously, Allport (1954) went on to describe attitudes as 'probably the most distinctive and indispensable concept in American Social Psychology. No term appears more frequently in experimental and theoretical literature.' This shows the dominance of research on attitudes within social psychology just over half a century ago. Although its influence has now declined, it is still one of the major research areas within social psychology.

The term attitude is derived from the Latin word aptus, which is also the root of the word aptitude, and indicates a state of preparedness or adaptation. Putting a psychological slant on this analysis, we can take attitudes as giving the person a subjective or psychological state of preparation for action. Most formal definitions of the term attitude include, either explicitly or implicitly, this notion of attitude as a state of mental preparedness. However, there are still substantial differences in the way different authors have elaborated on this basic notion. It will be instructive to examine a few definitions.

Definitions

It seems most appropriate to begin by considering what an attitude is. This may seem a rather odd question initially, as the term is in common use in everyday life. But that is precisely why we must define it, to give a very particular psychological meaning. In everyday life we may speak of someone as having an attitude. In reality we all have an attitude, many in fact! This is using attitude as an indicator of an antagonistic stance towards something, perhaps towards authority. Interestingly, in the eighteenth century the term attitude was used almost exclusively to denote a posture. No doubt artists would regularly ask their models to adopt a reclining attitude! Despite the fact that these terms do not clearly represent the psychologist's use of the term attitude, they do give us an insight into the psychologist's use of the term, and it is instructive to note how early notions have evolved as our understanding has grown.

Early definitions

One of the earliest definitions of attitudes, by Thomas and Znaniecki (1918), simply characterised them as 'a state of mind of the individual toward an object'. Here we see the basic idea of an orientation, or fitness for action. Note also the explicit mention of an object. Attitudes are always towards something. It could be a physical object, a person, or something more abstract such as giving to charity. It is often phrased as 'an object of psychological significance', to remind us that we don't have attitudes to absolutely everything, only those things that are relevant and important to us personally. Focusing on those aspects of our world that are important to us enables us to be economic with our limited cognitive resources.

Of course Thomas and Znaniecki's definition does seem to raise a couple of questions – such as what does 'state of mind' actually mean? And similarly, what determines which objects will become the focus of an individual's attitudes? A later definition by Thurstone (1931) gave at least some clarification to these issues. Thurstone defined an attitude as 'affect for or against a psychological object'. This still implies cognition to the extent that psychological objects are the focus of attitudes, but attitudes are seen as primarily affect or emotion. And this affect may be positive or negative. Interpersonal attitudes may be positive or negative, for example. We like some people and dislike others.

But we must, of course, acknowledge that ultimately attitudes are hypothetical constructs. Their existence cannot be seen or measured directly. We are only aware of people's attitudes through their behaviour. It may be behaviour we observe for ourselves or it may be the self-reports of the individual concerned. If I see you eating a chocolate bar I may assume that you have a positive attitude towards that particular brand of chocolate, and probably chocolate in general. Similarly, a statement of preference for some food is a verbal behaviour that reflects attitudes. Filling in an attitude scale is also a behavioural measure of attitudes. This does not itself constitute our attitude; it is simply a relatively quick and convenient way of enabling us to self-report our attitude in a given area. None of these expressions of attitude is direct; they each have their weaknesses as methods of assessing attitudes, but that will be discussed further in the next chapter.

A famous definition

Perhaps the most famous definition of attitudes is that of Gordon Allport (1954) who proposed that an attitude was 'A learned predisposition to think, feel and behave toward a person (or object) in a particular way'.

This definition is wonderfully economic in its language. Almost every word is crucial and worth explaining. First, note the word learned. This emphasises that attitudes are socially constructed; they are the result of experience; we are not born with positive or negative attitudes towards certain objects or groups. Until fairly recently most theorists would have argued that attitudes are learned – totally learned. Many social psychologists would still make this argument, but it is becoming increasingly untenable. Recent research is forcing social psychologists to acknowledge that the basis for some attitudes, or at least a predisposition to acquire them, may be biologically inherited. It is hard to deny that factors such as cognitive development or a predisposition to regard some objects as intrinsically fear-arousing may promote the development of some types of attitude, *but* this does not mean they are innate or inevitable. Experience is the ultimate determinant of attitudes.

The second major term in Allport's definition is predisposition. This is very important. This implies that attitudes pre-exist the object with which they are associated and actually bias responses to that object. At its simplest level this may be just that, a tendency to respond in certain either positive or negative ways. But it is also possible to take this as giving a much more directive role to attitudes, seeing them as a schema or framework through which the world is seen. An analogy I often make is that attitudes can be seen as like a window on the world. The form of the attitude determines what one sees, just as the frame around a window limits your view of the outside world and the potential interpretations you may make of what is happening. A nice example of this is the tendency of football supporters to see aspects of a match that confirm their own far from impartial attitudes. They are more likely to spot fouls from the opposition, and to spot good goal-scoring attempts from their own team!

The core of Allport's definition refers to what is sometimes called the triadic model of attitudes (discussed in detail later). The three components of the triad are affect, cognition and behaviour. This multi-dimensional view of attitudes makes a great deal of sense to most people: if we like something or someone (affect) we also tend to think positively about it or them (cognition) and are likely to either seek or avoid contact with the person or object. Note that Allport talks of these three elements as predispositions, signifying attitudes as some sort of latent process within the individual, something over and above a mere regularity in the individual's observed behaviour. In fact, the term predisposition is especially important because the three components of the model (especially the behavioural element) do not always seem to be closely linked. This has raised questions about the validity and viability of the triadic model.

Finally, the Allport definition says that attitudes involve *particular* responses. In other words, they involve cognitive, affective and behavioural responses that have some clear and specific association with the attitude object. They are also relatively consistent and enduring – an important aspect of an attitude if it is to have adaptive value for the individual.

A current overview

We have seen that the early approaches to defining attitudes may be grouped into two categories. One group of definitions sees attitudes as unidimensional, focusing on the affective or emotional response they entail. Thurstone's (1931) definition is a good, early example of this approach. A more recent example would be Ajzen and Fishbein's (1980) definition which sees attitude as 'a person's evaluation of any psychological object'. The second group represents a multi-component approach and typically gives equal emphasis to affect, cognition and behaviour. Allport's (1954) definition exemplifies this approach.

Both sets of theories recognise the importance of affect and, to a greater or lesser degree, cognition. A major concern with many modern theories is whether behaviour should also be included. Research has been inconsistent in finding a relationship between patterns of observable behaviour and the cognitive and affective elements of attitudes. At best, many authors are attempting to identify how this may be influenced by the strength with which an attitude is held, the impact of group norms, or the specific functions an attitude may serve for the individual (Maio and Olson, 2000; Petty and Krosnick, 1995; Terry and Hogg, 2000). At worst, a number of authors have been prompted to play down the idea that attitudes and behaviour are directly and strongly linked, and instead prefer to talk of a behavioural intention (Ajzen and Fishbein, 1980).

Research has been contradictory and has not resolved the issue of whether a unidimensional or a multi-dimensional definition of attitudes is most tenable. Some authors have been prompted to argue that it is too early to come down in favour of one view or the other (Chaiken and Stangor, 1987), while others have argued that dimensionality may vary according to the particular attitudes in question (Breckler, 1984). This argument has been going on for many decades and it still has some way to run.

Functions of attitudes

Although many authors have tried to delineate the psychological *structure* of attitudes, an alternative approach has been to identify them in terms of the functions they serve for the individual. Of course these are not necessarily exclusive – a given attitude may serve one or even several functions for an individual. Similarly, the functions that an attitude may serve for an individual may vary over time. So, for example, a teenager may express an attitude to initially gain entry to a desirable group but may subsequently use that attitudinal framework to evaluate other experiences and people. A number of functional theories have been proposed. They typically propose four distinct functions that attitudes can serve, although these may be named somewhat differently by different authors (Snyder and DeBono, 1989). Perhaps the best-known functional analysis of attitudes was proposed by Katz (1960). The four basic functions that he proposed were served by attitudes are described below:

The instrumental function

This has also been termed the adjustive or utilitarian function. Katz saw behavioural psychology as the modern expression of this function. Attitudes serving this function are helping the individual to maximise their rewards; they have some utility for the person. Perhaps liking a particular pop group or style of music makes you accepted within the social group that you belong to, and so holding and expressing this attitude will have a reward value for you. Of course this adaptive function of attitudes may be in the present or it may have been useful in the past and have simply persisted for the individual. For example, a child may have displayed prejudicial attitudes towards certain groups and these may have been affirmed by significant adults, such as parents. For a young child this parental validation may be extremely rewarding and so the attitude is strengthened. But this may be the start of a prejudicial attitude that can be very hard to overcome in later life, even though the reward it brings at that point may be non-existent or even negative. This raises an interesting point in terms of attitudes possessing reward value. In terms of behavioural psychology, one would expect attitudes that have been intermittently rewarding to be more strongly held than those that have been rewarded each time they are expressed! This may sound paradoxical but if you think about it a little the sense of this expectation becomes clear. As an example, some years ago there was a short film on the evening news which showed a demonstration march by an ultra-right-wing political group. To counter this there was an opposing march by a left-wing group. This news film showed the groups clashing and several scenes of individuals caught on their own being violently attacked by the opposing group members. Undoubtedly being beaten up by the opposition was not a positive, rewarding experience for the individuals concerned, but do you think this weakened their attitudes, whether right- or left-wing? It seems far more likely that it strengthened them, that the hapless victims had their antipathy to the opposing faction wholly confirmed and reinforced by the treatment they had received.

The ego-defence function

I have already said that attitudes may serve an adaptive function. They can give us an outlook on the world that protects us from harsh external realities, buffers our ego and rewards us. The attitudes we hold can help us feel good about ourselves. But if you follow this to its logical conclusion, they are also biasing our interpretation of the world. Within limits this is not likely to be significant, but if this self-serving bias and self-protection are taken to extremes then our perception of people, objects and events may be severely distorted and we may be psychologically very handicapped. Prejudicial attitudes are often held up as an example of attitudes serving an ego-defence function. The targets are created by the prejudiced individual, and their prejudices are likely to be intensified at times of stress and perceived threat to the self. For example, a person who has just been fired from a job is likely to feel even more prejudiced immediately after than before the event. This is not because there is any necessary relationship between the target of the prejudice and the prejudiced individual being dismissed from their job. It is simply that the minority group is being used as a scapegoat to support the individual's ego and self-esteem. Katz argues that Freudian and neo-Freudian psychology has been particularly concerned with this aspect of motivation and its consequences.

The value-expressive function

Attitudes may be significant for the individual because they support and are integral to their self-concept. Consequently, expressing and having these values and attitudes affirmed are a source of satisfaction to the individual. This is very evident to the parents of young teenagers! The teenage years are widely recognised as a time when the peer group becomes especially important in the life of the child (although many parents will be relieved to know that the extent of this is often exaggerated). It becomes very important for the teenager to achieve acceptance within their peer group, and so many attitudes are used to express this solidarity. These may be attitudes to music, styles of dress and a variety of other life-style factors. These attitudes may bring teenagers into conflict with their parents, emphasising that the value-expressive function is relative! Attitudes may serve to support self-image and aid group membership in some areas, but the values expressed may not be universally revered. This fact may be important to the holder of the attitudes, since attitudes can also be used to emphasise non-membership and distinctness from one group (e.g. independence from parents) as well as membership of another group (the peer group). Katz stresses that this function is of central importance to ego psychology (an extension of Freudian theory), although it would also seem to be highly applicable to humanistic psychology, such as Carl Rogers's (1980) Person Centred Counselling, which sees the self-concept as central to personal adjustment and happiness for the individual.

The knowledge function

The core idea of this function is that attitudes make our world more understandable. They provide a frame of reference for ascribing meaning to the things that happen to us and the things that we encounter. They help impose order on the world, make it predictable and help us feel we are functioning effectively. Of course the knowledge structures that we build up are not necessarily totally accurate, but they do provide us with a cognitively economical way of processing the vast amount of information that bombards us every minute of our waking day. Stereotypes are an example of knowledge structures that enable us to impose meaning on our world – they are the cognitive component of prejudicial attitudes. But stereotypes are often defined as faulty and inflexible generalisations (any broad generalisation is likely to be faulty, at least in parts, of course), and so we can see that the knowledge they do provide is at a price. Information can be more easily processed on the basis of a limited number of rules and characteristics, but the price of this lower depth of processing is that there may be some loss of accuracy. We may never process things to a sufficient depth that we realise that there are differences; people and situations may be hurriedly categorised as similar on the basis of just a few actual or assumed characteristics. We think we know the characteristics of the people we stereotype, but really we know only a few cues, the rest is inferred. Katz gave Gestalt Psychology as an example of a psychological approach stressing this function, because of its emphasis on the individual's search for meaning and structure in their world. In terms of more modern approaches, we can see this function exemplified in many cognitive and especially information-processing approaches to psychology.

Recent approaches

Although functional approaches have been popularly cited in the literature, they have received relatively little empirical testing (Shavitt, 1989). Some recent empirical research has, however,

11

provided interesting new insights on the approach. In a study by Shavitt (1990), three main attitude functions were identified: utilitarian, social identity and self-esteem maintenance. This essentially reduces Katz's taxonomy to three dimensions by combining the knowledge and instrumental functions into a single utilitarian function. More important than this difference in taxonomy, Shavitt also presents evidence that the success of attitude-change attempts may depend on the functions that the target attitude serves for the individual. In Shavitt's study advertisements were more likely to persuade when they were relevant to the function that the attitude was serving for the individual. However, Petty and Wegener (1998) argue that this effect may be due to the extra scrutiny that is given to persuasive messages that address important functions for the individual. In these circumstances, a cogent, persuasive argument may promote attitude change but a weak argument may actually inhibit it.

The concept of attitudes

So far in this chapter I have tended to talk about attitudes as if they are some very definite entity – albeit one whose nature is hotly disputed. It is appropriate at this point to note that this does not really do full justice to the very wide spread of interpretations of the nature and structure of attitudes. Two main approaches have been outlined in the study of attitudes: the probability and latent process approaches (DeFleur and Westie, 1963).

The probability approach is perhaps the least committed view of attitudes. It sees attitudes as simply a characteristic of certain patterns of behaviour, the *inferred* consistency of a response to an attitude object. So, for example, a consistently positive reaction to a certain person may be taken as indicating a positive interpersonal attitude to that person – that is, that you like them! We do not have to infer any deeper underlying process or cognitive structure. An attitude may simply be an inferred consistency in a response. Bem's (1967) Self-Perception Theory is a good example of this approach to attitudes, although most theorists do want to go beyond the immediately observable behaviour and infer some sort of mediating process.

Moving to the somewhat more theoretically committed view, the second group of theories has been termed latent process approaches. The latent process perspective extends the probability view by inferring some underlying process as the basis for the response consistency. It is this process rather than the behavioural consistency that is the attitude. The triadic model of attitudes is a good example of a latent process approach.

Major examples of both theoretical approaches to explaining attitudes are discussed in the next section.

Basic theoretical approaches

In this section I will focus on four basic approaches to attitudes: the classical or triadic model; Bem's Self-Perception Theory; the Subjective Expected Utility approach (a specific example of this approach – Ajzen and Fishbein's Theory of Reasoned Action – is dealt with in detail in Chapter 6); and a perspective from critical psychology that questions the very need and usefulness of a concept of attitude.

The triadic model of attitudes

You may have spotted an important difference in emphasis among the three definitions that I have outlined above. The first emphasised that cognition was central to the concept of attitude; the second placed emphasis on the emotional or affective component of attitudes; and the third emphasised behaviour. Many definitions have been based on the idea that attitudes are in fact a combination of all three of these elements. This approach has been called the classical or triadic model of attitudes. It sees attitudes as having three interconnected components (which are conveniently easy to remember because they begin with the first three letters of the alphabet):

Affect
Behaviour
Cognition

Affect, the emotional content of attitudes, can, of course, simply be seen as positive or negative, although it is also commonly scaled for significance, for degrees of affect. Cognitions are the perceived relationships between aspects of objects of psychological significance. For example, the cognitive element of our attitude towards a university education may be centred around our perception of a relationship between higher education and future occupational success. The behavioural element is simply the acting in accordance with our attitudes. If we like chocolate we probably also tend to buy it and eat it! Unfortunately we don't always act in accordance with our attitudes. Many factors may potentially inhibit the overt expression of an attitude. For example, prejudicial attitudes may not be expressed in some circumstances because the individual fears social disapproval and censure. Many modern theorists prefer to see the behavioural component as a predisposition, tendency or intention to behave in a certain way rather than as an overt act.

By now you are probably thinking that this model looks rather complicated – three components all supposedly being combined to produce this thing called an attitude. And you are probably wondering if these components are always in agreement. One would certainly expect them to be if they are supposed to be just three interrelated facets of the same psychological entity. Early attitude researchers had the same reservations and went to great lengths to investigate the consistency of these three components of the triadic model of attitudes.

Internal consistency

Research examining the relationship between the cognitive and affective components of attitudes has generally been supportive of them being closely connected. For example, in a famous study by Rosenberg (1960) it was found that if hypnotic suggestion was used to change the affective component of an attitude then there were corresponding changes in the associated cognitions. Although the unusual but admirably direct approach of this study has been criticised (for example, are good hypnotic subjects representative of the general population?), its findings are none the less fairly representative of the work in this area.

More difficult for the triadic model of attitudes has been the link between behaviour and the other components of attitudes. Some researchers have reported the required high correlation between attitudes and behaviour, but unfortunately others have found only poor relationship or even no significant association at all. Fishbein and Ajzen (1975) concluded that there was little evidence for a systematic relationship between attitudes and behaviour on a general level, and that specificity is required in levels of measurement. An example will clarify what is meant by this. A common defence to accusations of racial prejudice is that 'some of my best friends are black'. This is an example of measuring at different levels of specificity. The accusation is looking at attitudes to a group; the response concerns the attitude towards an individual. Can we really be surprised that behaviour towards an individual member of a group may show a poor correlation with attitudes towards the group as a whole? We should be more surprised when they do show a correlation. Even if we do measure attitudes and behaviour at the same level of specificity, many other factors may intervene to prevent the overt behavioural expression of an attitude. There may be an obstacle (for example, lack of money to purchase a desired object) or a time lag during which priorities and even attitudes may change, and a host of other competing attitudes may be aroused. In a review of 46 studies examining the relationship between attitudes and behaviour, Hanson (1980) found that 18 of the 26 laboratory studies did indeed find a positive relationship between attitudes and behaviour. In contrast, 16 out of 20 field studies did not find such a relationship. It appears that many more factors may intervene between attitudes and their behavioural expression in the real world than in the laboratory.

There have been several approaches to resolving the problem of consistency within the triadic model of attitudes. Some theorists have focused on specific elements to the exclusion of others; other theorists have even been moved to deny the concept of attitude and question its utility. The remainder of this chapter will give consideration to several of these alternative approaches to attitudes.

Self-Perception Theory

Perhaps one of the most extreme alternative views to the triadic model is to see attitudes not as some internal structure that guides behaviour, but rather the other way around, as something that individuals infer from observing their own behaviour. This view is most often attributed to Daryl Bem (1967), most commonly described as an unreconstructed behaviourist. Thus we may infer that we like wholemeal bread because we observe ourselves eating it regularly. The self-descriptions of our own behaviour can then become internalised self-instructions about ways to behave. This idea is not new, of course. It is essentially a variation of the James-Lange theory of emotions. Imagine you are in a field and a bull charges at you. What do you do? Most likely run away and feel afraid! In the James-Lange theory, the sequence follows that order – you run and so you feel a corresponding fear. This is the reverse of what many would assume – that you feel afraid and so run. Note the similarity to Bem's views on attitudes? Although this may sound an unusual approach, there is some evidence to support the view that emotions are at any rate partly – at least under conditions of ambiguity – determined by how we perceive the determinants of our physiological arousal. There is also some evidence that our attitudes are affected by self-observations. For example, if we give false heart-rate feedback to a person with spider phobia while exposing them to a spider, such that they believe their heart rate to be lower than it actually is, we tend to find that they report lower levels of fear than would otherwise be the case. The potential therapeutic use of this sort of phenomenon is obvious.

A more cognitive view of attitudes sees them as more influential in the early stages of perception, as templates actively guiding the way information is processed. Rather than attitudes simply being elicited by a stimulus, they are important in the interpretation of the stimulus. They are a template through which we construct our understanding of the world. So, for example, a racially prejudiced person does not simply respond to members of the prejudiced group but may be vigilant for cues to ethnicity and may interpret acts by members of the ethnic group differently from the same acts by other people.

Most modern psychologists do not believe in either extreme – in a purely cognitive or an extreme behavioural model of attitude. The most popular conceptions of attitudes are as combinations of affect and cognition. The Subjective Expected Utility (SEU) models that grew out of the earlier behavioural approaches have proved to be influential rivals to the traditional triadic model of attitudes and more recent cognitive and information-processing theories. It is to the SEU models of attitudes that I now turn.

Subjective Expected Utility models of attitudes

Building on behavioural ideas, SEU models see people as rationally attempting to maximise their anticipated positive outcomes and minimise their negative outcomes. Of course what you regard as a positive or negative outcome may vary (food to a hungry man is a positive outcome; it may be a negative to someone suffering the effects of food poisoning!). Hence subjective utility is stressed.

There are a number of variations on the SEU theme, perhaps the best-known being Fishbein and Ajzen's (1975) Theory of Reasoned Action. This splits the awkward behavioural component from attitudes (now composed of the remaining cognitive and affective components) and examines how attitudes affect behavioural intentions, which in turn are related to actual behaviour. From this view, a person's attitude towards an individual, object or act is essentially seen as the sum of that person's evaluatively weighted beliefs about the target. For example, a person's attitude towards higher education may be based on a number of beliefs. One central belief may be that a good education is associated with having a good job and a good income in later life.

The 'evaluative weighting' is simply how important this belief is to the person. Each of the major beliefs within an attitude could be given a weight according to its importance for that person, and the overall attitude would reflect the variety of beliefs and their relative importance for the individual. The most popular theory based on this approach – Fishbein and Ajzen's Theory of Reasoned Action – is discussed in detail in Chapter 6, where major approaches to attitude change and persuasion are examined.

Critical perspectives

In this chapter I started by mentioning Thomas and Znaniecki's approach to attitudes, largely to show how important the area has been within social psychology as a discipline. What I did not discuss was their ideas about the social nature of attitudes. In their view, attitudes are the 'glue' that meld people into groups, and give them a social identity and status. This tradition has largely been continued within sociological social psychology, while mainstream social psychology, dominated by American influences, has increasingly come to stress the role of the individual rather than the broader society or community to which the individual belongs. Of course, these two perspectives are not exclusive. Indeed, one could argue that to have a full understanding of attitudes (and other social psychological phenomena) one needs to appreciate their complexity on both an individual and a wider social level. One needs to understand the ways in which people are similar as well as the things that make them different and unique. In the previous sections of this chapter I have outlined in some detail the dominant, individualistic approach to the study of attitudes. It is now appropriate to consider critiques and alternatives to this approach, largely produced by European social psychologists.

No social psychologist would deny that attitudes are to a very large extent socially acquired. Attitudes may be constructed either directly from experience or from our observations and interactions with others. If our beliefs are socially constructed they are to a substantial extent also shared with other members of our community. Our way of thinking, our social representations, are a reflection of those of the wider social group to which we belong. Evidence in support of this idea can be found both in developmental studies that show children's social representations of their community to become clearer with age (Augoustinos, 1991), and in studies that show that levels of social involvement correspond with the details and organisation of an individual's social understanding (Pryor and Merluzzi, 1985).

Discourse analysts, emphasising the role of language in social behaviour and cognition, have severely criticised the traditional concept of attitude, and especially the means by which attitudes are typically assessed. Potter and Wetherell (1987) raise three major objections. First, they argue that attitude objects are often vaguely and far from neutrally defined. For example, if we are assessing attitudes to 'coloured immigrants' then this is actually glossing over the vagueness of the term 'colour' and whether immigrant status is cognitively differentiated from 'non-immigrant' by the respondent. Second, both the question we ask to elicit attitudinal data, and the way we transform such data when it is gathered, mean that perhaps the end product is as much a reflection of the researcher as the respondent. Do attitude scales and questionnaires really do full justice to the richness and complexity of attitudes? Finally, attitudinal research makes the crucial assumption that there is some underlying, relatively permanent entity that is being tapped – the attitude. Attitudes are seen as having some neutral, objective status rather than being linguistically constructed in response to a specific social context. But in different situations or at different times we may sometimes express very different attitudes. Because of these inherent problems with the traditional conceptualisation of attitudes, and methods of assessing them, discourse analysts adopt a fundamentally different approach and, rather than trying to ascertain some underlying cognitive entity, are more 'interested in the different ways in which texts are organised, and the consequences of using some organisations rather than others' (Potter and Wetherell, 1987). Because there is no assumption of an underlying attitudinal entity, there is no expectation that an individual will necessarily be consistent or coherent in the attitude statements they espouse, except to the extent that there is consistency in the functions of the discourse.

Summary

This chapter introduced the basic concept of attitude. Defining attitudes was problematic in that any definition must reflect the underlying nature of the object being defined, and there are major theoretical disagreements about the nature of attitudes. Definitions emphasising affect and cognition were discussed, and the influential triadic model, combining affect, cognition and behaviour, was outlined. A number of alternative theoretical approaches to attitudes were then outlined: the functional approach, Bem's Self-Perception Theory and the Subjective Expected Utility approach. The final group of theories discussed were critical of the whole concept of attitude and argue for a broader social perspective. Rather than looking for cognitive structure within the individual, they see attitudes as being derived from the individual's social context and organised by language.

Further reading

Augoustinos, M. and Walker, I. (1995) *Social cognition.* London: Sage. Contains a good introductory chapter on the psychology of attitudes and two excellent chapters expounding post-modern challenges to traditional social cognitive approaches.

Eagly, A. and Chaiken, S. (1993) *The psychology of attitudes.* Fort Worth, TX: Harcourt Brace Jovanovich. A detailed review of current research on attitudes.

Potter, J. and Wetherell, M. (1987) *Discourse and social psychology: beyond attitudes and behaviour.* London: Sage. Contains a brief but very useful section introducing an alternative way of looking at the psychology of attitudes.

Origins
of attitudes

Introduction

A S WE HAVE SEEN FROM the previous chapter, attitudes are complex entities. With such a complex phenomenon it should come as no surprise that attitudes can be acquired in many ways. Perhaps because of this, and because we are continually exposed to situations that provide us with attitudinal information, it is little wonder that people often seem to hold contradictory, multi-faceted attitudes that take on different hues from one time or situation to another. The fact that attitudes may be acquired in a variety of ways, emphasising either the cognitive or affective elements, also has significant implications for what is likely to be the most effective strategy for persuasion. Persuasion is generally more effective if it matches the cognitive or affective significance of the attitude for the individual (Fabrigar and Petty, 1999).

In this chapter I will outline seven major ways by which we can develop or acquire attitudes. Although I present these separately for clarity of discussion, they do not work in isolation and will often complement each other. So, for example, instrumental conditioning can serve to strengthen or weaken existing attitudes and behaviours, but it needs something to work on. In contrast, classical conditioning and observational learning may be useful ways of acquiring an attitude where none existed before. It is obvious that these processes can work well together to initiate and promote the development of an attitude.

Although these theories are also major explanations of attitude change, a number of major approaches have been developed specifically to explain the effects of persuasive communications. The interested reader should refer to Chapter 6 for further detailed information on these approaches.

Informational influences

In discussing the nature of attitudes I have examined the triadic model, and you will recall that this consists of three components: affect, behaviour and *cognition*. Cognition essentially is the knowledge element. But this model was not alone in highlighting the importance of knowledge. Katz (1960) discussed a knowledge function for attitudes, and Fishbein and Ajzen (1975) outlined a model of attitudes as evaluatively weighted beliefs. All of these approaches are telling us that if we affect a person's beliefs we are also likely to be affecting their attitudes. One way in which we gather information is through out direct experience (discussed in the next section); the other is through various forms of communication, including the mass media. In this section I will examine two ways in which attitude information can be communicated: through person-to-person communication and via the mass media.

Personal communication

All behaviour has communication value. Even if you sit still and do not move a muscle, you are communicating – albeit that maybe you want to be left in peace! To the extent that people are bombarded with communications all day long, it would be naïve to assume that these have no attitudinal impact. Indeed, personal communications may be a particularly potent source of attitudes on several counts. First, they are difficult to avoid! If you disagree with or are not interested in the views expressed on the TV you can switch it off. This is somewhat more difficult with another person – especially if that person is someone important to you such as a friend or a family member. Second, we deliberately seek out and use others as sources of attitude information. Perhaps you have a friend who is particularly knowledgeable about politics and follows political events closely? It may be easier to form your opinion of some political event after chatting to that person rather than going to read all the political propaganda and counter-propaganda first hand. This is the two-step flow theory of communication (Katz and Lazarsfeld, 1955). It suggests that there are opinion leaders who actively engage with the mass media and that many of us acquire information second hand through these well-informed individuals. These opinion leaders are supposedly distributed throughout the social network and will differ according to the topic of concern. A group may have one opinion leader for politics and perhaps another for football. Although this theory has been criticised, it and other empirical research do emphasise that second-hand information can be important as a basis for the formation of attitudes (e.g. Maio *et al.*, 1994). It is also a useful reminder that attitudes are social objects and part of a negotiated social reality.

Mass media

Information from the media has long been recognised by the general public as a major factor in attitude formation and change, and also as an influence on behaviour. Amongst academics the picture is viewed less simply. For example, the impact of the mass media on attitudes to aggression and actual aggressive behaviour has been a subject of great controversy, with hundreds of research studies having been conducted (Erwin and Hough, 1997). The argument has tended to become polarised, with some people arguing that the mass media do affect attitudes and aggressive behaviour, and others arguing exactly the opposite, that they do not. In fact, it seems highly likely that the mass media have a considerable effect on some people, almost no effect on others, and varying degrees of effect between these two extremes on the majority of people. The role of psychology is to determine the factors that cause these variations in impact, rather than to reduce the argument to such a simple level that it becomes virtually meaningless and impossible to prove either way.

In Chapter 5, I shall examine in detail some of the characteristics of messages that may make them more or less effective as agents of attitude change and persuasion. At this point it is useful simply to note the message content and patterns of communication that are presented to us by the mass media. The media may reinforce, shape and challenge our attitudes in a number of areas, ranging from the social roles of men and women, to racial stereotyping, and social issues such as education, crime and the health service. Sometimes these influences are obvious to us. More often they can be subtle and insidious and largely go unnoticed.

One area that has received substantial attention is the way gender roles are presented in the mass media – how men and women are portrayed. Television has received the greatest research attention. Television advertisements have typically reinforced, and seldom served to challenge, traditional sex role stereotypes (Manstead and McCulloch, 1981). Traditionally when women featured in advertising they were likely to be portrayed as homemakers (perhaps in connection with home products), in a child-care role, as secretaries and personal assistants in industry, or in typically female stereotyped professions such as nursing. Their physical appearance and attractiveness were often regarded as being of major importance and emphasised. Research has shown that exposure to attractive women in advertisements can increase body dissatisfaction in women (Lavine et al., 1999). Distortions and misevaluations of body image play a substantial role in anorexia, and anything that contributes to these biased perceptions must be treated with concern because of the impact it could have on certain vulnerable sections of the population. In contrast, men in adverts are likely to appear as authority figures, experts, bosses in industry, and in major professional roles such as doctors. Although there has undoubtedly been some erosion (and even reversal in some adverts) in gender stereotyping in advertising over the last couple of decades, sex role stereotyping remains universal in television advertising around the world (Furnham and Mak, 1999).

Although advertising may obviously build on existing stereotypes as a means of getting its messages across quickly, almost as a form of shorthand (Hadjimarcou and Hu, 1999), it is far from being alone in the gender images it projects. Television programming of all types may be seen to convey similar messages.

The media do not influence our attitudes simply through providing us with specific message content to learn. They may also have an impact through a phenomenon known as agenda setting. This is where topics are made salient and hence we are likely to discuss and think about the issues raised. This may be sufficient to form or change our attitudes in those areas. This is particularly evident in news programmes, where reporting specific incidents or issues brings them to the forefront of our attention. When we hear about moves to ban activities such as fox hunting, and the protest marches in support of or against such activities, then we may or may not be persuaded by either side, but we are at least likely to think about the issues involved. British television news claims to strive for objectivity (though one may want to consider the extent to which this is truly possible), but this is certainly not the case in all countries, and not the case in British newspapers. On this count the potential impact of all aspects of the mass media and the messages they convey should be of concern to all of us.

Direct experience

Perhaps the most obvious origin of attitudes is in our direct experience. How many of us encountered school semolina and instantly developed a negative attitude towards that dessert that lasts us the rest of our life! In similar but more serious vein many negative attitudes may be the result of a direct traumatic experience. An aversion to dogs may result from the experience of having been previously bitten by a dog. And, of course, positive experiences could give us a corresponding push to developing positive attitudes. Maybe the child who is taken to football matches and finds these enjoyable will develop a positive attitude towards the sport and become a supporter in their own right in due course. Although there is no denying the significance of direct experience as a basis for acquiring attitudes, it is not really a full theoretical explanation and several processes may be implicated. Undoubtedly these direct experiences may provide a context in which we can acquire attitudes through social learning and the various other behavioural and cognitive processes outlined in the other sections of this chapter. But there are also some other distinctive processes that need to be considered. In this section I will discuss the fact that we tend to have more positive feelings about familiar objects and are more wary of the unfamiliar – the mere exposure effect – and how direct experience may promote the development of attitudes through the opportunity it provides to gather information.

Mere exposure

One of the simplest sources of attitudes is through mere exposure to the attitude object (Zajonc, 1968). The mere exposure effect is well documented in a number of areas. For example, we tend to like people whom we see regularly, even if we do not interact with them (Moreland and Beach, 1992). In fact, the mere exposure effect does seem to work best with relatively unobtrusive stimuli, and it may be that when we pay close attention we make additional inferences and a variety of additional cognitive processes come into play. Mere exposure effects are undoubtedly important factors in the effectiveness of many much-repeated advertisements, and perhaps the fact that we tend to pay relatively little attention to most adverts emphasises this effect.

Although mere exposure seems most influential with unobtrusive stimuli, it does, nonetheless , have an impact even with familiar, everyday objects. In an ingenious experimental demonstration of this, Mita *et al.* (1977) took photographs of women and either printed them in the standard way (so presenting an image of the subject as others see them), or as a mirror image (as the subject would see themselves in a mirror). These photographs were shown to the women and their friends. The majority (68 per cent) of participants preferred the mirror image of themselves, whereas the friends preferred the standard photographs. These preferences reflect their exposure to these different images. We normally only see ourselves by reflection, and our friends see us through direct perception.

Despite the evidence in favour of a familiarity-liking effect, a positive attitudinal outcome is not inevitable. Before you rush out to use it to improve your social life we should note a couple of qualifiers to the effect. First, if we begin with an initially negative attitude to an object or person, then continued exposure may serve to increase that negativity (Warr, 1965). Most homicide victims know their killers! A second factor limiting the impact of the mere exposure effect seems to be boredom (Bornstein, 1989). It is possible to have *too much* exposure. Continued re-exposure will ultimately result in a decrease in liking. Many advertisers get around this by creating advertisements that represent variations on a theme, attempting to get the benefits of familiarity while avoiding boredom. The boredom effect also seems to be influenced by the complexity of the attitude object. We seem to tire of relatively simple objects much more quickly than more complex objects (Sluckin *et al.*, 1980). Fortunately for our personal relationships, people are extremely complex attitude objects and we have some degree of control over our levels of exposure.

Actual contact

Actual contact and direct experience of an attitude object are a major, powerful way in which we gather information and test our beliefs. Unfortunately, direct experience of or tests of our attitudes are not always possible or practical.

The importance of direct experience and situational factors in attitude formation is well documented in the research literature. An example is the famous Robbers Cave study (in case you are wondering, Robbers Cave is the name of a State Park in Oklahoma) by Sherif *et al.* (1961). In this fairly complex experiment, the children attending a holiday camp were split into two groups (the 'Rattlers' and 'Eagles'). After these groups had had time to become established they were introduced to each other for the purposes of engaging in a series of competitive games with points and prizes at stake. Fairly rapidly, the groups became extremely hostile and antagonistic towards each other. Subsequently, this proved quite hard to reverse. It seemed that the major way of reversing this antagonism and promoting positive inter-group attitudes was through the use of superordinate goals; these were goals that required the co-operation of the two groups if they were to be achieved. The moral of the tale is clear: direct experience is seldom an objective gathering of information, and the context of that experience must be taken into account.

Despite Sherif *et al.*'s experiment, many early attempts to promote interracial harmony and integration were based on the idea that much prejudice arose out of ignorance, and if people only knew the members of the other racial groups then prejudice would be reduced. Unfortunately many of these well-meaning early attempts failed because they were too simplistic. Simply arranging a work or social environment to force contact ignored the fact that people and groups do not just occupy space – they interact and form relationships, and the nature of these interactions and relationships may be a crucial determinant of whether contact with the other group is evaluated positively or negatively. Enforced contact between two antagonistic groups is unlikely to promote positive inter-group relations if they perceive themselves as in competition for scarce resources; it may well *increase* hostilities and negative stereotyping. Yes, it may allow the gathering of information, but people may select information that reinforces their existing ideas about the other group, and selectively interpret the behaviour of the out-group to confirm their existing notions. In other words, in some situations continued exposure may simply enable us to gather further confirming evidence to support our initial position. In contrast, and as shown by Sherif's study, situations that encourage contact under conditions of interdependence, co-operation and shared goals are much more likely to lead to positive interpersonal perception and attitudes. And to the extent that groups are seen as homogeneous and an individual as typical, positive attitudes are more likely to be generalised from the individual group member to the group as a whole (Brown *et al.*, 1999).

Classical conditioning

This form of conditioning emphasises that the context in which we experience a neutral object may determine the attitude we develop to that object. Classical conditioning emphasises the importance of the association of some neutral stimulus object with a response evoked by some other stimulus that has some sort of emotional or affective value for us. The most famous example of this, known to many people even outside of psychology, is Pavlov's dogs. In his study of their digestion Pavlov would feed his dogs with meat powder (the *unconditioned stimulus*) and this would lead to a natural reflex production of gastric juices (the *unconditioned response*). But what Pavlov also noted was that other neutral stimuli came to be associated with this unconditioned reflex. So, for example, the sight of the approaching experimenter or the sound of his footsteps (*conditioned stimuli*) also began to evoke some fraction of the unconditioned response, gastric secretions. This was termed the *conditioned response*. Now if I re-present the above description using social stimuli and outcomes then the significance of classical conditioning for attitude acquisition will become evident. To do this I will look at interpersonal attitudes. More specifically, I will use an example from the social psychology of interpersonal attraction. Byrne (1971) showed that similarity of attitudes was a good predictor of interpersonal attraction. We tend to like people who hold similar attitudes to our own. He explained this in terms of a classical conditioning model. Byrne argued that similar attitudes have a reward value for us because they allow us to engage in social comparison (see the section later in this chapter) and thus confirm our view of the world and that we are functioning realistically and effectively in it. Thus we like the similar attitudes. In our social relationships, attitudes do not exist in a vacuum. They are held by people, and so, to the extent that a person is associated with the similar attitudes, that person will evoke some fraction of the positive evaluation generated by the similar attitudes. So, in this illustration, the similar attitudes represent unconditioned stimuli, the positive evaluation of these is the unconditioned response, the person holding the attitudes is the conditioned stimulus, and the liking that we develop for that person is the conditioned response – a fractional component of the positive evaluation resulting from the attitude similarity effect. Of course even the unconditioned stimuli in this example are not grounded in biological reflexes as basic as those observed by Pavlov. Many attitudes are undoubtedly built on quite complex patterns of conditioning.

Although I have given just one fairly simple example of classical conditioning as a basis for attitude acquisition, it is likely that its impact is pervasive and perhaps largely goes unnoticed. For example, many advertisements may try to evoke good feelings in us through the use of music, humour, attractive scenes, or attractive actors and actresses, on the basis that associating a product with the positive feelings these evoke may result in the product itself being more favourably evaluated. In similar vein, we often see advertisements on racing cars and on the walls of sports stadiums, again trying to associate the product with the positive feelings evoked by the sport and the excitement of the competition. The attitude towards the advertisement itself is related to the attitude to the product and intentions to purchase it (MacKenzie et al., 1986).

Subliminal conditioning

Although much classical conditioning may well occur at a very obvious, conscious level, there is some evidence to suggest that we may also be influenced by stimuli that we may not be aware of. In a study by Krosnick et al. (1992), participants were shown photographs of individuals engaged in everyday activities, such as shopping or getting into a car. Unknown to the participants, these photographs were preceded by other photographs that were presented at a speed that rendered them below the level of conscious awareness. These subliminal stimuli would typically evoke either positive or negative feelings in the participant. For example, a positive subliminal image might be of a person laughing while playing cards, and a negative subliminal image might be of a surgical operation. When attitudes to the stranger were subsequently assessed, the group exposed to the negative subliminal images reported much less positive evaluations than those exposed to positive subliminal images. The researchers did check that the experimental participants did not detect the emotionally loaded subliminal stimuli, and this confirmed that the conditioning was achieved without the awareness of participants. It appears that our attitudes can be influenced without our awareness. The topic of subliminal persuasion is a controversial one. It has been argued that you can evoke an existing attitude or predisposition but that you cannot change an attitude (Larson, 1992). However, the evidence from Krosnick *et al.* does also suggest that new attitudes may be affected by subliminal conditioning – and this may be a lot more common than we think.

Instrumental conditioning

This approach emphasises the role of reinforcement in the acquisition and maintenance of behaviour. If we regard attitudes as evaluative responses or behaviours (whether internal or overt), then we can see the relevance of this theory as an explanation for the development and maintenance of attitudes. Instrumental conditioning emphasises the fact that behaviours (and attitudes) that are rewarded will tend to grow stronger, and those that are not will tend to be superseded by the increasingly strong rival behaviours. In this context, a reward may be either some event that is positive for an individual or the cessation of something that is negative. Conversely, responses followed by a negative consequence are likely to decrease in frequency and strength. For example, giving a child a sweet or praise (a symbolic reward) for some positive act is likely to reinforce that behaviour and its associated attitude. Instrumental conditioning is an important means by which parents shape their children's attitudes in a number of areas – towards issues such as education, religion, various social values, hygiene and so on. It can of course reinforce negative as well as positive attitudes. A prejudiced parent may signal approval when their child expresses prejudicial attitudes, and may voice agreement and may even give tangible rewards when the child expresses a bigoted point of view similar to their own. It seems that young children of only 2 or 3 years of age may have the ability to categorise others on the basis of ethnic and gender labels, but acquiring and applying stereotypes and evaluative judgements seem much more dependent on the socialisation experiences of the individual, and on the patterns of reward for expressing such judgements. And of course once these attitudes are acquired, the individual is likely to find it most rewarding to associate with others who hold similar attitudes, providing a continual re-affirmation and reinforcement of their point of view (see the section on social comparison processes). Although instrumental conditioning may be especially potent in shaping the attitudes of young children, it affects us all throughout the whole of our lives.

The nature of rewards

Before finishing this discussion of instrumental conditioning it is important to mention a couple of technical matters. First, you may have noted in my first example, above, that I said giving a sweet or praise was *likely* to reinforce a response. It does, of course, depend on whether the child regards parental praise as rewarding or whether the child finds it more rewarding to annoy its parents! I make this point to emphasise that it is sometimes difficult to pre-determine what will be rewarding for an individual. A sweet may be rewarding, but anyone who has worked in a sweet factory will tell you that they stopped their initial non-stop eating of sweets fairly soon after starting there. A second important point to note is that we can only reward behaviours and attitudes that already exist. We can shape and strengthen behaviours rather than create them, although we may acquire the initial behaviour or attitude through some of the other processes discussed in this chapter, such as direct information, classical conditioning or observational learning. Finally, a great deal of research in behavioural psychology has been devoted to ascertaining the most potent patterns of reward in order to change behaviours. Although we do not have time to deal with this topic in depth (and research has largely been in areas other than the psychology of attitudes), it is important to note that the number, patterning and timing of reinforcements can have a substantial impact on conditioning.

Observational learning

Observational learning – sometimes called modelling or vicarious learning – is a theory about how we may learn attitudes and behaviour by observing the attitudes and behaviour of another (usually called the model) and its consequences. These models may be live or symbolic (e.g. in the mass media). It is important to note that this type of learning, unlike classical and instrumental conditioning, does not rely on extrinsic rewards (Bandura, 1971). Undoubtedly this is a major source of attitude learning. From very early in childhood we acquire information by observing parents, siblings and friends, teachers and other significant individuals, or through watching television.

Modelling may have at least three main effects on the individual: informational, motivational and reinforcing. The informational impact we have largely covered already, in the earlier section on information gathering. Less obvious perhaps are the other two functions of observational learning. In observing behaviour we also learn its potential usefulness or value to us. This may serve to encourage or discourage the expression of the behaviour under specific circumstances. The child who observes another child being punished for some antisocial behaviour may be less inclined to engage in that behaviour themselves. As to the final, reinforcing function of observing a model, we may well, of course, have encountered some variant of the observed attitude or behaviour before, and in these circumstances our observations may serve to confirm or weaken the perceived link between existing attitudes or behaviours and their consequences. To illustrate this, let me elaborate on my previous example. Do all children who engage in antisocial behaviour get punished by their parents, or do some individuals actually gain benefits in some way? Maybe a child throwing a tantrum in the supermarket receives some sweets to keep them quiet . . . an interesting lesson for the child in question and potentially for any other child that observes the event. They are learning that they can use public tantrums to hold their parents to ransom and receive desired rewards.

The process of observational learning

Four main factors affect the observational learning of behaviour and attitudes: attention, retention, reproduction and motivation. To learn or change an attitude, one first has to be aware of its existence. Television advertisers are well aware of this and may use catchy tunes or humour, short scenes and fast-moving action to grab the viewer's attention. People are also more likely to pay attention to models that they can identify with. In the case of young children the model may be a parent. Later in life it may be peers, especially those of the same sex, and figures in the mass media or admired individuals. Once we have given our attention to the behaviour or communication, we have to process the information to which we have been exposed. Although some theories of persuasion do stress that some forms of persuasion can occur with minimal cognitive processing, observational learning stresses that to learn a whole new attitude or behaviour does require that the new information be encoded and retained. The more cognitive processing that occurs, the more firmly grounded the attitude is likely to be. These two stages are crucial in the acquisition of an attitude, but the third crucial stage is the reproduction of the attitude or behaviour. Do we act on and express the attitude or behaviour? As we shall see in the next chapter, the link between attitudes and behaviour is tenuous at the best of times. A whole variety of circumstances may intervene to prevent the expression of the attitude, or the individual may simply be insufficiently skilled or motivated to reproduce the learned behaviours. Complying with a persuasive message may entail a cost as well as a benefit to the individual. The final stage in Bandura's model of learning is reinforcement. Note that it is the expression of the behaviour that is affected by reinforcement rather than its initial learning. Reinforcement may be by some direct consequence of the act; or by indirect consequences, perhaps by observing some other individual engaging in the act and being rewarded or punished; or because it has some internal value for the individual or the individual has learned to provide self-reinforcement for the act. This latter approach is something many counsellors have to teach clients in order to maintain the changes brought about during therapy.

35

Pervasive impact of observational learning

There is substantial research evidence to support Bandura's theory of observational learning. It has been demonstrated in children with live and symbolic models. It is widely used in counselling and clinical psychology. Millions of pounds each year are spent on advertising in which a model receives some tangible or social reward, or self-esteem reward, for purchasing and using a specific product or engaging in some behaviour, such as giving to a charitable appeal. Through these mechanisms, amongst others, the mass media are undoubtedly exerting a significant impact on a great many people's attitudes. No doubt the advertisers wish they could have as much impact on people's behaviour!

Social comparison

The theory of social comparison processes was proposed by Leon Festinger (1954) and basically argues that there is an innate drive to evaluate our attitudes and abilities. This makes considerable sense in that it would be hard to function effectively if we were operating on the basis of erroneous information. In line with this, it appears that the drive for social comparison is higher in those areas where we are less certain of our standing and at times of uncertainty. Perhaps this partly explains the great need for adolescents to form groups and simply 'hang out' together. Although they appear to be doing relatively little, in reality they may be conducting a major comparison of their attitudes, attributes and social standing within a rapidly expanding social world.

Many beliefs can be objectively tested. I can test whether I can run a marathon by actually attempting the feat. But many other beliefs and attitudes cannot be tested objectively, and under these circumstances we may have to resort to an indirect method, social comparison. For example, how can you test whether you are good at running the marathon? Only by comparing your performance with that of other people. This sort of comparison does not provide you with an objective validation of your beliefs and attitudes, but it does provide you with a *consensual validation* –

validation based on a social consensus. Many of our most important abilities and attitudes are social in nature and cannot be objectively tested, and so the consensual validation provided by the social comparison process is extremely important to us. Social comparison of attitudes, for example, has been seen as being of such importance that it at least partially explains why we affiliate with individuals with similar attitudes – to get the consensual validation of our attitudes, the affirmation that we are functioning effectively in our social world (Byrne, 1971). You may have spotted the slight catch in the consensual validation argument: it is really just a test of whether someone else has a similar set of attitudes to yourself; it is not really a test of how functional and adaptive those attitudes are. It is quite possible that two individuals may have a similar set of maladaptive attitudes.

The related attributes hypothesis

Festinger's initial paper on social comparison processes has spawned a lot of subsequent research. While it constitutes a very impressive starting point, aspects of it were also to prove to be vague and difficult to test. For example, if we strive to make social comparisons by seeking similar people with whom to compare ourselves, are we really 'testing' our attitudes or are we merely seeking to have them confirmed regardless? Also, how do we find similar others for comparison purposes? It is a bit of a chicken and egg situation in that we cannot know a person is similar until we have made a comparison, and by then it is too late if they are dissimilar. One potential solution to this dilemma has been termed the *related attributes hypothesis* (Goethals and Darley, 1977; Miller, 1984): maybe we search out comparison figures who are similar to us in certain important ways (perhaps age, gender and so on), and then compare on the crucial attitudes (music, fashion, parents, etc.). Potentially, the greater this similarity, the more credence we are likely to give to the results of the social comparison process, although sometimes it also seems that the similarities we used as the basis for selecting our comparison figures may actually have little or no real relationship to the attitudes or abilities being evaluated. For example, school pupils may evaluate their performance in different curriculum areas on the basis of what they perceive as a typical level of performance for their gender, rather than the more general standard of the norms for their age group as a whole. Perhaps they have different expectations for science subjects in comparison to arts subjects. These more limited comparisons may potentially have significant implications for motivating or de-motivating academic performance.

Social comparison may serve a number of goals for the individual and hence function differently in different circumstances (Wood, 1989). For example, if we are motivated by self-improvement, perhaps in some sporting ability or desire to join some social group, we may make comparisons with others who are superior to us on that ability or who are members of the admired group (an *upward comparison*). Likewise, if we are motivated to enhance our self-esteem we may make comparisons with others who are inferior to us on some ability (a *downward comparison*). Social comparisons are hardly the unbiased process originally portrayed.

While a similarity on related attributes may be a useful basis for evaluating (and possibly modifying) existing attitudes, it may also underpin the development of new attitudes. To return to my original example of the adolescent group, on initially joining such a group teenagers may start by comparing themselves and their values with other group members and the group values as a whole. They may find they admire some individuals and take on some of their attitudes and behaviours. If they are attracted to the group they may start to compare it with other groups and form attitudes about these other groups that create a psychological distance between the groups and confirm their choice of group in preference to the alternatives.

Heredity

The traditional definition of attitude was that it was a learned predisposition. More recent research, albeit relatively few studies at the moment, suggests that this may not always be the case. There may be a genetic basis for the development of at least some attitudes. Intuitively this does make sense, if you think about it carefully. It has long been known, for example, that some phobias (e.g. phobias about snakes and spiders) are more easily acquired and hence more common than others, so it would seem to follow that we may also be predisposed to develop negative attitudes towards these creatures. Similarly, some aspects of personality appear to have genetic roots and it would seem logical that people with certain types of personality may be more inclined to develop and hold certain types of attitude. For example, perhaps an extremely anxious person may be more likely to develop various fearful attitudes?

Once we start accepting that there may be some sort of genetic basis for at least some attitudes, it is not going that much further to hypothesise that individuals who are more closely related (i.e. more genetically similar) would be expected to have more similar attitudes in those areas where there is a genetic component. It is important to note that I am saying there is a genetic component or basis, a predisposition to develop some attitudes – definitely not that attitudes are innate! The potential mechanisms behind any genetic impact on attitudes are still far from clear.

The typical procedure to study the magnitude and effects of heredity on psychological attributes (including attitudes) is to compare individuals of varying degrees of relatedness. It is especially common for studies to focus on twins. Twins may be identical, coming from the same fertilised egg, and hence are referred to as monozygotic, or else they may be non-identical, coming from two separate fertilised eggs, referred to as dizygotic. In the former case the twins are genetically identical, in the latter case they are not. Through examining the similarities and differences between such pairs we can get an insight into the extent to which genetic factors impact on the psychological characteristics of the individual. What may be even more useful is to include in the comparison sets of twins who were reared together in the same environment and those who were reared separately. This allows some consideration of the impact of environmental factors.

Taken together, examining monozygotic and dizygotic twins who were reared either together or apart, gives us a substantial insight into the extent of genetic and environmental influences on the psychological characteristic being investigated.

What little direct research evidence there is certainly does seem to support the view that heredity does indeed contribute to the development of attitudes. Identical twins are more likely to have similar attitudes than non-identical twins. This effect is not simply because identical twins are raised under similar conditions; it is evident even in twins separated early in life and raised in quite different environments.

The impact of heredity on attitudes does appear to differ according to the attitudes concerned. It is more significant in certain fairly basic attitudes that emphasise affective or emotional elements, such as musical preferences, rather than attitudes that are more cognitive or intellectual in nature, such as those towards more abstract issues or in areas where the individual has little direct experience. For example, one study suggested that religious attitudes may be moderately influenced by genetic factors, whereas the decision as to which religion to join may be largely determined by social and cultural influences (Donofrio *et al.*, 1999).

Anecdotally, twins that have been parted early in life but then meet up later often report a natural rapport. Perhaps this can be explained at least in part by the research on the heritability of attitudes. That similarity of attitudes may underpin liking and social contact is well known, but it also appears that there may be a genetic basis accounting for at least some of the attitude similarity effects (Posner *et al.*, 1996). It also appears that those attitudes that are higher in heritability may be responded to more quickly, more resistant to change and more significant in the attitudinal similarity-liking effect (Tesser, 1993, 1998).

Summary

This chapter examined seven major ways in which attitudes may be acquired. At the very simplest level we may gather information directly and base our attitudes on this. The mass media have received a lot of attention for their potential significance in this regard, although personal communication, actual experiences and even mere exposure to attitude objects may also have an impact. Behavioural theories stress the role of rewards and punishments in the learning of attitudes, while observational learning stresses that we can learn attitudes by simply observing others, although rewards are seen as important determinants as to whether these learned attitudes and behaviours will be expressed. Social comparison theory stresses the importance of comparing our attitudes and opinions with those held by other people, which may lead to changes. Finally, I examined the role of heredity in attitude formation. There is increasing evidence for a genetic component to some attitudes, especially these concerned with simple, affective responses. The overall picture was that we have many complex, interconnected ways of acquiring attitudes.

Further reading

Perloff, R. M. (1993) *The dynamics of persuasion.* Hillsdale, NJ: LEA. Contains a good chapter on attitude formation – with special attention given to subliminal persuasion.

Tesser, A. (1993) The importance of heritability in psychological research – the case of attitudes. *Psychological Review, 100,* 129–142. Essential reading for those who still think all attitudes are learned; it provides good evidence for an element of heritability in some attitudes.

Wood, J. V. (1989) Theory and research concerning social comparisons of personal attributes. *Psychological Bulletin, 106,* 231–248. A useful review of developments since Festinger's original formulation of social comparison theory.

Chapter 3

Measuring
attitudes

Introduction

ALTHOUGH ONE CAN THEORISE about the nature of attitudes as a hypothetical construct, to be of practical value we need to be able to measure them in some way. In this section I will put the huge range of approaches to measuring attitudes into a few major categories and briefly discuss some of the issues that have underpinned their development. The remainder of this chapter will examine the individual categories of approach and major techniques in more detail.

As you might expect from an area of psychology that has been around for so long, a great many methods have evolved. The great diversity of approaches has undoubtedly been driven by the wide variety of research questions that psychologists are interested in, as well as the creativity and individuality of researchers. So, for example, if you are interested in the attitudes of a large population to some relatively innocuous issue such as which supermarket they prefer, you will want a relatively quick and easy-to-administer method which, ideally, would not require too much expert supervision. A survey or standardised attitude scale may be the ideal solution here. On the other hand, perhaps you are interested in measuring very sensitive attitudes, maybe towards prejudice and discrimination. These sorts of attitudes are very prone to faking and people giving socially desirable responses. To combat this, you need either to disguise your purpose, if you want to use attitude scales, or perhaps to come at the important issues indirectly. Maybe instead of using an attitude scale you could use a much more subtle, indirect technique such as a projective test. Of course if people do fake their attitude responses it is often to save face, so one method of guaranteeing a genuine rather than socially desirable response is to lead people to believe that faked responses can be spotted. If they can be convinced of this, then they are pressurised into revealing their true attitudes rather than appearing either to be a liar or to have no self-awareness. Quite a bit of research has looked at this, though one might consider that this could be ethically dubious under some circumstances.

As you may have gathered from the above discussion, the effort that has been devoted to measuring attitudes in a relatively formal way has been considerable, but some researchers have adopted totally different approaches to get over some of the problems of the formal approaches. One strategy is to approach the problem of attitude measurement in the reverse way to that adopted by the formal methods. Instead of devising some highly structured instrument or technique to which people provide responses, why not elicit the responses informally, perhaps through an interview or diaries they have been asked to keep, and then seek to establish their attitudes towards a topic through analysing their responses? Although the construction of attitude scales involves a lot of work, they are very easy to mark and process subsequently. In contrast, informal methods of attitude measurement can sometimes be very quick to put together, but they can also involve considerable labour in processing the gathered information to ascertain the respondents' attitudes.

The techniques mentioned above have focused in the main on people reporting their own attitudes in some way or another, with varying degrees of formality and directness. There is, of course, a way that does not rely on self-reports: direct observation of behaviour. Although you might be thinking to yourself that this is a more objective approach, this also has its conceptual and practical problems. On a practical level, one can't observe all of a person's behaviour all of the time, so deciding what to observe, when, and how to categorise it is a major problem. On a more conceptual level, if attitudes are an essentially subjective phenomenon, are we managing to tap into that by taking this 'objective' measure? As I discuss in the next chapter, the relationship between attitudes and behaviour is certainly very far from being totally consistent. Many research careers have been built on demonstrating precisely that fact!

So where does this take us? The bottom line is that there is no ideal or perfect way of going about measuring attitudes. The choice of which approach is most appropriate for any particular assessment of attitudes will depend both on the issues under investigation and on the populations concerned. Some issues, such as prejudice, discrimination and illegal or socially disapproved-of acts, may require a more subtle approach than other issues where individual variation is more socially accepted. Similarly some populations, such as children, the elderly and the disabled, may require approaches that take account of their cognitive or physical ability to participate. The attention span and reading ability of young children and the physical or mental abilities of various disabled groups must all be taken into account if they are to fully participate in attitude studies. To give more detailed consideration to some of these issues in attitude measurement it is now appropriate to examine the various approaches in more detail. First, we will look at the most widely used approach, formal attitude scales.

Observing behaviour

Although this may appear the most obvious and direct method of assessing attitudes, it is also, perhaps less obviously, one of the most complicated approaches. For a start, it makes the rather major assumption that we behave in ways consistent with our attitudes. As we shall see when we examine this issue in detail in the next chapter, this is far from always the case. A variety of factors may intervene to prevent a simple, clear relationship between attitudes and behaviour. A few quick examples will make this clear. Social pressures may mean that we feel unable to express attitudes that are counter to a group norm; we may fear marginalisation or even expulsion if we express deviant attitudes. Or it may be that we hold certain attitudes, perhaps towards some commercial product, but none the less we do not buy it. Why? Maybe it is more expensive than the one we do buy, or our local shop does not stock it and it would be inconvenient to go to shops that do stock it. Although not hard research evidence, these rather obvious examples are testimony to the fact that we do not always behave in accordance with our attitudes. I am sure that you can think of examples where this is evident even in your own behaviour.

Despite the above examples, it is also a truth that we do behave in accord with many of our attitudes. So what, you may ask, is the problem with assessing these through the direct observation of behaviour? The short answer to that question is that it is actually very difficult to observe behaviour accurately and systematically. To put a little more detail on this answer, let's look at some of the difficulties. The first difficulty we are likely to encounter in attempting to infer attitudes from behaviour comes from the fact that behaviour is continuous. Even standing still doing nothing is behaviour. So we need some way to divide up the behaviour stream. It would be difficult to observe everything all of the time. So maybe we would decide to sample the behaviour. We could watch a person for one longish period of time, but that could have problems as well. Maybe the behaviour that reveals the attitude is not exhibited all the time but only intermittently. So, unless we are going to make our single observation for a very long time indeed, maybe we would be better off with a number of shorter periods of observation with intervals between them. But that doesn't seem to get over the problem of where we are going to make our observations. It may well be that the attitude-relevant behaviours are only evident under certain circumstances. For example, what if we are interested in interpersonal attitudes, specifically liking, among schoolchildren? If we were to observe them in a formal school classroom, where seats have been allocated, we might conclude that two individuals do not show liking towards each other. However, were we to observe them in the playground we might discover that they spent a great deal of time together and even appeared to be best friends. So where they were observed could be crucially important for that attitude. We could try having a 'standard situation' in which people were observed, but is this true to real life? Would the results have any true meaning in relation to how and when attitudes are expressed in the real world? There are no easy answers. At the very least it seems we have another factor to take into account when making our observation of attitudes: attitudes may be situation-specific. And the complications do not stop there. In the preceding example I talked about liking and interpersonal attraction. You may well have noticed that I did not specify what exactly was being observed to allow an inference of liking and friendship. Behaviour can be ambiguous and difficult to interpret. Very often, observational studies will use a series of categories to observe patterns of behaviour (e.g. Bales and Cohen, 1979). Such systems can be complex to use and require considerable training to use effectively, and they do not of themselves eliminate possible biases resulting from the preconceptions and expectations of the observer. One possible solution is to have more than one observer and look at the extent to which they agree on what they observed – how they categorised specific behaviours. This certainly goes some way towards resolving possible observer bias, but even a good level of agreement that certain behaviours were observed still does not give meaning to those behaviours. That requires interpretation, some form of inferential leap on the part of the researcher.

Even assuming we can resolve all the difficulties discussed above, we still have to consider the impact our observations may have on the person being observed. If a person is aware that they are being observed they may alter their behaviour. They may behave in a socially desirable way, go to the opposite extreme, or even respond directly to the observer.

Overall, behavioural observation of attitudes does have many virtues; it does at least allow you to discover when, where and how specific attitudes achieve expression. But it is not an easy way to assess attitudes, and for many purposes alternative approaches may be quicker and more effective. In particular, attitude scales are often resorted to for a quick snapshot summary of a person's attitudes on a particular topic. It is to attitude scaling that I turn next.

Attitude scales

Attitude scales have a number of advantages and disadvantages. In terms of advantages, a psychological test is typically used because it is a relatively simple and efficient means of gathering information. Attitude scales are simple in that all the respondent has to do is typically either tick a relatively small number of statements (often referred to as items) to indicate agreement, or else rate those statements on, for example, a 5- or 7-point scale. They are efficient in that it is possible to test large numbers of people fairly rapidly and cheaply, with minimal expert supervision. A respondent's score on an attitude scale will place them at some point along a continuum for the attitude being assessed; it shows both the direction of their attitude (positive or negative) and its relative strength – how positive or negative it is. A big bonus in the eyes of many researchers is that the numerical data from attitude scales can be subjected to statistical analysis.

Despite the many advantages of attitude scales, there are also, unfortunately, a number of serious disadvantages. First, there is one massive assumption that I have already mentioned in passing: the assumption that a score derived from a response to an attitude scale accurately reflects the respondent's actual attitude. Characteristics of the scale, including how well it is constructed, may distort responses. Social pressures may also impact on the responses to an attitude scale. The respondent may seek to either give the researcher the results they think he or she wants; or perhaps the opposite may apply – antagonistic respondents may deliberately try to give misleading answers. Even if we are willing to assume that the scale is well constructed and the respondent is answering truthfully, we are still left with the assumption that attitudes are consistent, can be quantified and that it is appropriate to measure them on some sort of unidimensional, linear scale. You may wish to ask yourself if all your attitudes fit into this neat little description. I'm pretty sure not all mine are that clear-cut! These issues hark back to the differences of opinion between psychologists on the nature of attitudes, which were addressed in Chapter 1. Many researchers are unwilling to make such assumptions and prefer a much less rigid view of the nature of attitudes, which necessitates that they must assess them by some other means.

As we shall see, though, attitude scales are not easy to construct and there are complex issues relating to their reliability (the extent to which the scale would give the same result if a person were to be re-tested) and validity (the extent to which the scale measures what it purports to measure). Although there are a wide variety of attitude scaling methods that you may come across, the most common are Thurstone scales and Likert scales, and so I will examine these in some detail. I will give a brief account of the procedures used in the construction of Thurstone and Likert scales, to give an insight into the amount of labour involved in constructing an attitude scale (not something to be entered into lightly!). I will also mention, in substantially less detail, some other somewhat more complicated approaches to attitude scaling that you may come across in your reading.

The Thurstone scale

One of Thurstone and Chave's (1929) main concerns was to establish an attitude scale in which the items were at equally appearing intervals, from an extreme negative point through to an extreme positive point. That is, that to the respondent each item appeared to be an equal amount more positive than the previous item and an equal amount more negative than the next item. Not unsurprisingly, this method of attitude scaling has been termed the method of equally appearing intervals. In appearance, a typical Thurstone scale consists of a series of attitude statements, and the respondent's task is simply to indicate agreement or disagreement with each item. Note that respondents cannot indicate levels of agreement with the attitude statements – they must simply agree or disagree. Compare this with the approach of the Likert scale, which we will discuss in the next section. For an example of the format of a Thurstone scale, an attitude scale about dogs might contain items such as:

1　A dog is a person's best friend
2　Having to walk a dog encourages people to take exercise

3   I would keep a dog if it did not take so much time to take
     care of it
4   Poorly controlled dogs are a public nuisance
5   Dogs are dirty and unhygienic

These items are just meant to be an example. There would typically be many times this number of items (perhaps twenty or more
items, although substantially shorter and longer scales than that
are not uncommon). From the process of scale construction, which
we will examine shortly, each item would already have been
assigned a value in terms of the attitude in question. Typically
this will be between 1 and 11. Once a respondent has indicated
which items are agreed with, the median value of those items (the
middle value from the set of statements that the respondent agreed
with) is the respondent's attitude score. For example, if our
respondent agreed with items 2, 3 and 5 and these had prede-
termined values of 5.5, 4.5 and 2.0, respectively, then the median
value and hence the respondents' attitude score would be 4.5.
Although respondents are only expected to agree with a small
number of items on a Thurstone scale (the others will be either
too positive or too negative to get their agreement), it should be
very evident to you that by taking the median score of the statements that are agreed with we are reducing the likelihood of
extreme attitudes.

It is worth noting at this point that, although a Thurstone
scale is linear, we must be careful about treating scale values as
'real' numbers. A score of 6 would indicate a more positive attitude than a score of 3, but it would not indicate an attitude that
is twice as positive. The scale values represent a rank ordering
rather than actual numbers that are additive on a linear scale.
You may recall that we are dealing with equally *appearing* intervals, a psychological concept, rather than actually equal intervals.

Constructing a Thurstone scale

1   The first stage in the construction of any attitude scale is the
     collection of a large number of attitude statements. Typically
     100–150 statements may be used. These are not as easy to

collect as you might imagine, but too few at this stage will just lead to problems later on, when there are insufficient reliable statements to represent the full range of attitudes in the area of interest. Edwards (1957) lists a set of fourteen criteria for well-written attitude statements. Any that are obviously ambiguous, irrelevant, or non-discriminating should be eliminated. Insufficient attention to this point could result in the scale having to be abandoned at a later stage, after a great deal of time and effort has already been expended. So, at the very beginning, it really is worth the extra effort to get as large a pool of well-constructed attitude statements as possible.

2   The next stage of scale construction consists of getting a number of 'judges', representative of the population for whom the scale is intended, to rate the statements on an 11-point scale. If it is meant for students, then have student judges. If it is meant for middle-aged businessmen, then have them as the judges. Any obviously biased individuals, with extreme, entrenched attitudes, are excluded as these tend to bunch towards either the top or bottom end of the scale. For better or for worse, this group of individuals then constitute our unbiased judges. Typically there may be 40 or 50 judges, although many more than this have sometimes been used. Note that judges are not expected to give their own opinions (hence eliminating obviously biased individuals from the panel of judges); rather they are expected to try to give their objective evaluation of the statements. They have to try to ignore their own agreement or disagreement with the items. You may wish to ask yourself the extent to which you think such unbiased evaluations are possible in practice.

3   Each statement is given a value equal to the median (i.e. the middle value) of all the ratings given by the judges.

4   Statements with high levels of agreement between the judges are selected (as these appear to be evoking more consistent, reliable responses).

5   From the pool of consistent statements a series of items are selected that are spaced at approximately equal intervals

through the range of the attitude scale. So, for example, we might have items with ratings of 1.0, 1.5, 2.0, 2.5, etc.

6   Hey presto! We have our scale and can now administer it, although we may still wish to collect more substantial evidence as to the scale's reliability and validity.

A detailed discussion of the complex issues of assessing the reliability and validity of psychological tests is beyond the scope of this book, but I will touch on them briefly as they are of crucial importance in scale construction (see Anastasi and Urbina, 1997, for more detailed information).

Reliability is concerned with the extent to which a test will give roughly the same results were a person to be re-tested. It can be assessed in a variety of ways, ranging from simply testing and re-testing a group of subjects, to various statistical procedures. Reliability is an important prerequisite for validity, although it does not itself guarantee validity.

Validity is concerned with whether the scale does actually measure what it purports to measure. Initially the scale constructor may argue in terms of face validity (that the scale looks as if it is measuring the attitude of interest). Our item analysis will also have produced a basic content validity (an assurance that each item is measuring the same thing). As evidence accumulates, a more substantial claim for validity may be made by reference to the scale's predictive validity – its power to predict future behaviour – or its concurrent validity – its association with some other scale or criterion measure. For example, if we did construct a scale about attitudes to dogs then we might regard a correlation between dog ownership and high scores on our scale as providing some evidence of validity.

The Likert scale

Despite the huge advance represented by the development of the Thurstone scale, it has been overtaken in popularity by the Likert scale, sometimes known as the 'method of summated ratings' (Likert, 1932). Part of the reason for this popularity is that a

Likert scale may be up to 30 per cent quicker to construct than a corresponding Thurstone scale, and yet the two scales correlate well (Edwards and Kenny, 1946).

Likert scales take the form of a series of statements that are rated on a 5-point scale. Taking the first item from the Thurstone scale example above, here is what it would look like in Likert format:

1 A dog is a person's best friend

Strongly agree	Agree	Undecided	Disagree	Strongly disagree
1	2	3	4	5

Many students in their practical work and projects will often use a scale in this Likert format, although it is worth noting that simply presenting a statement in this rating scale format does not make it a Likert scale. The construction of a proper attitude scale requires that consideration be given to issues of reliability and validity.

As with the Thurstone scale, a Likert scale would consist of a number of items. Respondents have to rate each item for level of agreement. The overall attitude score from a Likert scale is obtained by adding together the ratings from each individual item (hence the term 'method of summated ratings').

Constructing a Likert scale

In devising his method, Likert had two main concerns: first, that his scale should be *unidimensional*, i.e. that all the items were measuring the same thing; second, Likert's method of scale construction sought to eliminate the need for judges. You may recall that the construction of a Thurstone scale required unbiased judges and that I commented on the difficulty of this notion. The construction of a Likert scale simply requires the initial pool of attitude statements to be rated by a relatively large group of individuals according to their own beliefs and evaluations.

The actual procedure for constructing a Likert scale consists of a relatively straightforward series of steps:

1   The collection of a large pool of initial items. The same guidelines apply as with Thurstone scales as to what constitutes a well-written item. In particular, it is advisable not to have too many neutral or very extreme items (Oppenheim, 1992).

2   The initial set of attitude statements is given to a trial group of, say, 100 respondents who are representative of the sample for whom the scale is intended. Some scale constructors have used substantially more respondents. The respondent's task is simply to indicate their agreement with each of the large group of initial scale items, using a 5-point scale, as outlined above.

3   The scale is now subject to a process of *item analysis* to reduce the large initial pool of attitude statements down to the required final number of items. There are a large number of methods of item analysis – perhaps the easiest and certainly the most common is by means of comparing item-total correlations. To do this we calculate each respondent's total score on the draft scale and then correlate their rating of each individual item on their scale with that total score. In fact, to be totally accurate, we should be correlating each item with the total score *minus* the value of the item being evaluated; correlating an item with itself does undoubtedly bias item-total correlation. In practical terms, this very slight difference in procedure usually has very little impact on the outcome of an item analysis, and it is often considerably easier and quicker to calculate simple item-total correlations – especially if the calculations are not being done by computer.

The above method of item analysis may seem rather strange at first, but if you remember that our aim is to get a set of items that are all measuring the same thing you will begin to see how it is achieving this. The correlation coefficient is a measure of agreement between two variables. A high correlation would tell us that an item is rated low by individuals who score low on the overall scale but high by individuals who score high on the scale. In other words, the item is predictive of the overall attitude score on the scale and hence is likely to be measuring the same thing as the other items on the scale.

Through this item analysis we can reduce our pool of items substantially. We may be left with a set of perhaps 10 to 20 items with a relatively high internal consistency, and, to that extent, they possess at least a basic sort of validity. More detailed assessments of reliability and validity would follow the patterns outlined in the discussion of the Thurstone scale.

4   Our scale is now ready to administer. Unlike the Thurstone scale, items have no intrinsic scale value other than that ascribed to them by the respondent who rates them for agreement. An individual's attitude score is the sum of their ratings of each individual scale item. And now, after reading the details of construction procedures for a Likert scale, you can see why I say that simply asking research participants to rate a statement does not mean that the rating scale qualifies for the title Likert scale!

Other methods of attitude scaling

Researchers have been very creative in developing a wide range of attitude scales. Other common approaches that you may come across are social distance scales (Bogardus, 1925) and Scalogram analysis (Guttman, 1950). I will say just a few words about each of these approaches. More detail can be obtained from Oppenheim's (1992) excellent book.

The social distance scale is extremely simple, but has intuitive appeal. It typically presents a range of possible alternatives of varying levels of positivity, and the respondent simply indicates those with which he or she agrees. For example, if we were interested in prejudice we might ask a respondent to indicate the extent to which they would be willing to enter into relationships of varying degrees of closeness with the individual. These might range from working alongside that person, through to being a member of the same club, through to kinship by marriage. Although this scale does allow a simple ordering of respondents with regard to their attitude on the issue of concern, its psychometric properties have been severely criticised and this may limit its more general usefulness. More sophisticated versions of this scale have been proposed which may give it more general utility.

Scalogram analysis is a complex technique. The end result of a laborious scale construction method is a test that contains a list of items in rank order. Respondents tick all the items they agree with, and this means that they should be ticking all items up to a certain point and then no further. The implication of this is that if we know someone's score on such a scale then we also know precisely which items they agreed with. This is in contrast to the Thurstone and Likert scales where two people could score exactly the same on a test and yet have agreed with quite a different set of statements. Scalogram scales can be quite short and yet effective for measuring even quite small changes in attitude.

The bogus pipeline technique

This technique was developed by Jones and Sigall (1971) in response to concerns about social desirability effects in attitude studies, especially common in studies of ethnic prejudice. People (especially in student populations) may not want to appear prejudiced and intolerant of ethnic minorities in the very liberal context of a college or university; hence they may give socially desirable rather than true responses to an attitude scale. One rather ingenious way to get around this social desirability effect has been called the bogus pipeline technique. The basic idea behind this approach is that the person whose attitude is being assessed is led to believe that the researcher has some sort of direct insight into their actual attitude, whether or not they express it overtly. In fact this 'pipeline' into the research participant's actual attitude is bogus, but the mere fact that the participant believes it may be possible should spur them to be truthful when questioned about their attitudes. After all, they don't want to appear to be a liar or lacking in self-awareness as well as prejudiced!

As will be evident from this description, the whole technique rests on the extent to which the participants in the research can be successfully convinced that the researcher does actually have access to their real attitudes. To convince them of this, the participant typically is confronted with a complex set of machinery and told that it is similar to a lie detector. They are wired up to the machine using standard electrodes and there are probably flashing lights and obvious signs that the machinery is busy at crucial times. They are also given a trial run at trying to deceive the machine by answering some simple questions, typically based on fragments of information they have revealed in a prior questionnaire. As this information will have been noted and secretly passed to an experimental assistant who actually controls the machine, it is simple for the machine to appear to be able to see through any deceit on the part of the participant. With the participant suitably convinced that it is impossible to deceive the machine, the researcher can question them as to their attitudes on the real topic of interest.

Bogus pipeline techniques have been shown to be successful in encouraging the disclosure of potentially sensitive information in a number of areas, ranging from prejudicial attitudes through to dieting failures, sexual behaviour, excessive smoking, drinking, drug use and other socially undesirable behaviours (Aguinis et al., 1993; Mulheim et al., 1998; Roese and Jamieson, 1993; Tourangeau et al., 1997).

The bogus pipeline technique obviously involves a great deal of effort on the part of the researcher, and to this extent it may be too cumbersome and expensive to use except in limited circumstances where socially desirable responding is highly likely. One somewhat less cumbersome variant of the bogus pipeline procedure is not to actually connect the respondent to the machine but simply to introduce them to the apparatus and indicate that it *may* be used to check their responses at a later time. This approach seems to be just as effective as using the full bogus pipeline procedure (Roese and Jamieson, 1993).

Despite its apparent success, the bogus pipeline technique has been severely criticised on a number of counts. One major drawback is the deception involved (Aguinis and Handelsman, 1997). Nowadays psychologists prefer not to use deception unless absolutely necessary. Sigall (1997) has defended the deception involved on the grounds that it is comparable to other psycho-logical research that may also use deception. But this deception may be doubly undesirable on the count that it is also going to be increasing the respondent's level of stress. This is almost inevitable given the purpose of making them reveal information that they may otherwise have preferred to keep concealed. These considerations may again limit the usefulness of the technique to situations where the benefits of the research can demonstrably justify such an intrusive approach.

Informal approaches

In this category I place the wide variety of methods that, while they do typically involve self reports in a variety of guises, do not use formal scaling methods and often have a broader perspec-tive than can be summed up in a single attitude score.

In this section I include various survey instruments, check-lists and rating scales, diaries and sociometry. I will examine each briefly in turn.

Surveys

Survey methodology is a huge topic in itself and many books have been written in this area. Surveys are less common as a research tool in psychology than in some of the other social sciences. We are all aware of this form of attitude assessment from the various opinion polls that are routinely taken to tell us of one political party or another's rising success or deepening distress. Questions may take many forms, ranging from the fixed-choice (requiring the selection of one of several fixed alternative answers) through to the open-ended (giving the respondent the freedom to respond with their own ideas in their own words. Of course, the more open questions are, the more difficult they are to analyse, but open-ended questions do arguably give us a richer, more detailed insight into a person's unique attitudes.

Checklists and rating scales

Checklists and rating scales are similar to the closed-style questions that may be part of a survey. They are essentially variations on the same theme, but where the checklist is asking the respondent to indicate simple agreement or disagreement with a statement, the rating scale allows them to indicate degrees of agreement. Checklists and rating scales can often be fairly easily constructed, but the effort and attention that is expended in putting them together will be an important factor in determining the usefulness of any data gathered with them. A pilot study to check on wording, their appropriateness to a particular target group, and potential demand effects (cueing the respondent in to the responses that may be sought by the researcher) may help iron out many problems. Although checklists and rating scales have the appearance of rigour, they can be very uncontrolled devices and may have poor reliability and dubious validity. At the very least, respondents are only reacting to the items as presented, and they may give socially desirable responses, or at least the responses they think the researcher wants. We do not know if the items in these scales are the only (or even the major) issues that the person considers relevant to the topic concerned. Are the responses predictive of behaviour, and to what extent would we get the same responses if we were to re-test the individual? With rating scales we also have the additional problem of the *meaning* of the various ratings. If we are using a 5-point scale, does this run from positive to negative, or is it just one side of the continuum? Similarly, what do the various points on the scale imply? Does the middle point signify ambivalence, neutrality or simply no attitude? There may not even be a middle choice if we use four or six points on the scale. This would force the respondent to make a decision one way or the other. These issues must be clearly thought through and spelled out to the people completing the scale if there is to be any chance of equivalence between different respondents, or even if the researcher is to have any idea of what a given score implies in terms of attitudes.

Diaries

Diary studies are a useful way of obtaining a longitudinal record of a respondent's activity over a period of time that may range from a few hours up to possibly several months – provided respondents can be persuaded to keep such a regular record. Diary studies are regularly used to examine things such as patterns of variation in mood, clinical conditions and social activity (e.g. Keefe, 2000; Nezlek, 1999). One interesting variation on this technique is to issue the participants with telephone pagers, and they are required to complete the diary whenever the experimenter calls them (e.g. Gauvin *et al.*, 1996). I suspect that those calls sometimes come at awkward and embarrassing times!

The diary technique is better suited for recording behaviour than attitudes, and as the next chapter in this book suggests, there is not always a good link between attitudes and behaviour. Diary studies can be expensive and, as the respondent will be completing the diary independently, we may be unaware of a varying tide of outside influences that may affect the record from one time to another.

Sociometry

Moreno (1953) is typically cited as the founding father of sociometry, although similar techniques had been in use by other researchers somewhat earlier. Basically, sociometry is a method of assessing the interpersonal attitudes and popularity (attractions and repulsions) within a group. It typically requires the naming (or sometimes rank ordering or rating for preference) of group members who satisfy certain criteria. For example, schoolchildren may be asked to nominate those members of their class who are their friends, or to list in order their preferred playmates within the class. Moreno has argued that the limit of the group of eligibles should be specified (e.g. the classroom group) but that the number of choices an individual is allowed to make should be unrestricted, limited only by the number of group members who fit the criterion. On a practical note, it does also make the task easier for the respondent if we impose as few restrictions as possible. In fact, research indicates that the earlier, more readily elicited choices are more likely to be the better friends and are more consistently volunteered if the respondent is re-tested. More recent research has also suggested that sociometric studies should look not only at positive choices within the group (attractions) but also repulsions. The negative aspect of social choice tends to have been somewhat neglected, possibly because of the sensitivity and practical difficulties of eliciting such information.

Sociometry is a generally useful and interesting technique for studying attitudes in a specific, limited domain – that of within-group interpersonal preferences – but care must be exercised as to how it is used. Most importantly, care is needed in what you ask in your sociometric question, how you phrase it and how you ask it. For example, asking children who are their best friends may elicit different responses compared with asking them who they play with most. Similarly, young children may be better able to cope with the technique if they are presented with photographs of the field of eligibles that they can point to, rather than being asked to remember and to speak or to write down their responses.

Projective approaches

Under this heading I will discuss some of the huge variety of approaches that have been used to infer a person's attitude from their responses to some apparently unrelated, minimally related or ambiguous task. From these tasks we may gain an insight into a person's fantasies and associations and the general way individuals are disposed to interpret their world. Projective tests may allow the investigator to side-step some of the barriers that may ordinarily inhibit the expression of an attitude, such as the pressures to give socially desirable, rational responses (Livneh and Antonak, 1994). They may also be able to tap into responses below the respondent's own level of awareness. As examples, they may be especially useful where the attitude of concern is a sensitive one, such as prejudice, where people may be unwilling to disclose their genuine attitudes, or if we are trying to assess attitudes at some deeper, perhaps unconscious, level. They may be especially suitable for examining self-attitudes, stereotypes and prejudice and can be useful exploratory tools.

Projective methods generally work by requiring the respondent to categorise objects, fantasise, free associate or respond to ambiguous stimuli. The most well-known projective methods require the respondent to tell stories around or interpret the content of a series of ambiguous pictures (the Thematic Apperception Test) or inkblots (the very famous Rorschach Test). Other approaches on the same sort of lines may require respondents to fill in the speech bubbles in cartoons, complete unfinished sentences or stories (e.g. 'When I go to the dentist I . . .'), interpret the behaviour of characters in stories, or judge pseudo-facts (e.g. the proportion of the population that is from an ethnic minority).

Although these various approaches do potentially allow a level of insight into a person's attitude that may go beyond that in most formal attitude scales, it is at a cost. That potential cost is the reliability and objectivity they may lack. These approaches have been criticised because different investigators can give quite different interpretations based on the same set of responses.

Summary

This chapter examined the issue of measuring attitudes. Most methods assume that attitudes are some kind of enduring, relatively invariant cognitive structure that can be measured on a continuum. Four main approaches were outlined: direct observation of behaviour, formal attitude scales, informal approaches and projective techniques. Each was noted as having advantages and disadvantages in terms of ease or difficulty of development, use and interpretation. A recurring theme throughout the chapter was the issue of the relative reliability and validity of the various ways of measuring attitudes – that is, would they produce the same results if the respondent were re-tested, and does the test really measure what it purports to? Also of concern is the extent to which the various methods of assessment limit or even determine the scope and nature of the measured attitude.

Further reading

Anastasi, A. and Urbina, S. (1997) *Psychological testing* (7th edn). Englewood Cliffs, NJ: Prentice-Hall. The book to go to for all matters concerned with psychological testing.

Eagly, A. and Chaiken, S. (1993) *The psychology of attitudes*. Fort Worth, TX: Harcourt Brace Jovanovich. Although a general graduate-level textbook, chapter 2 is devoted to the measurement of attitudes.

Oppenheim, A. N. (1992) *Questionnaire design, interviewing and attitude measurement*. London: Heinemann. The latest edition of a classic text. A readable and comprehensive introduction to a fragmented and complex area.

Chapter 4

Attitudes and behaviour

Introduction

IN THE FIRST CHAPTER OF this book I mentioned one of the major thorns in the side of attitude theory: the often poor link between attitudes and behaviour. This is an important topic and so I will examine two main elements of it in this chapter.

First, I will examine the extent to which attitudes are reflected in our overt behaviour. To be a really useful concept we need to understand the link, but it is very clear that there is no simple relationship. Whether we conceptualise attitudes as having a behavioural component or see them as simply predictive of behaviour, we do need to understand the factors that may strengthen or weaken the association and increase our ability to predict a person's behaviour on the basis of their attitudes.

My second theme for this chapter builds on the idea of a close association between attitudes and behaviour, but examines it from a somewhat different perspective. Typically, studies of persuasion look at how behaviour may change when attitudes are changed, but a great deal of research has also examined the converse – the extent to which individuals may alter their attitudes to fit in with their behaviour when their behaviour is counter-attitudinal.

Attitudes and overt behaviour

The link between attitudes and overt behaviour has been a controversial issue since the very early days of social psychology. To review this topic in detail, I will examine some of the early research in the area, and then look at more recent contributions to the debate that have helped clarify the questions, as well as suggest answers to the problems identified.

The La Piere study

This is an extremely famous and much-criticised study. Despite the many criticisms, it will be instructive to examine this study for three main reasons. First, published in 1934, this was one of the earliest studies to question the attitude–behaviour link, and so it provides a useful foundation on which to build this discussion. Second, our critique of this study will highlight some of the methodological and conceptual issues that have to be addressed to explain the attitude–behaviour link. Finally, I want to examine this study in detail because it is evident from some texts that it is a much-reported piece of research whose details often seem to become blurred in the repeated telling of the story.

This study began in 1930 when La Piere spent a period of two years travelling extensively within America with a young Chinese student and his wife. In the course of these travels they visited 67 hotels, auto-camps and 'tourist homes', and 184 restaurants and cafes. Although this was a time of considerable prejudice towards oriental people in the United States, they were refused service only once – in 'a rather inferior auto-camp'. La Piere noted that if they received extra attention at all, it was generally positive.

Six months after the period of travelling, La Piere sent a questionnaire to the various establishments that he had visited. Included in the questionnaire was the crucial question 'Will you accept members of the Chinese race as guests in your establishment?' He ultimately managed to get completed replies from 81 restaurants and cafes and 47 of the accommodation venues. La Piere reported that 92 per cent of eating establishments and 91 per cent of the accommodation venues answered no to the crucial question. All but one of the remaining responses was 'uncertain; depending upon circumstance'. One auto-camp owner replied in the affirmative. In his discussion La Piere concluded that questionnaires are poor indicators of social attitudes and that the assessment of such attitudes 'must, in the main, be derived from a study of humans behaving in actual social situations'. However, the study is more commonly cited as evidence for a poor link between expressed attitudes and behaviour.

Criticism of the La Piere study

As I indicated at the beginning of this section, this study has been much criticised, and I shall briefly mention some of these criticisms before moving on to look at more recent research and opinion on the attitude–behaviour debate.

Perhaps the major criticisms relate to the questionnaire procedure used in this study. First, one must ask oneself whether on receiving such a questionnaire one would feel that it was almost prompting a negative response. Would people really be sending a questionnaire to simply find out that anyone and everyone is served? Certainly it seems to be trying to access a general stereotypic response. Maybe this is why only about half of the establishments replied to the questionnaire even after La Piere showed 'persistence' to get them returned. Perhaps the other establishments were not willing to answer a questionnaire that seemed to require them to stereotype whole groups of people?

The methodology of this study also highlights a common theme that has emerged in the study of the link between attitudes and behaviour – the level of specificity of each. The questionnaire that was sent to the various establishments asked about Chinese people in general. What stereotype does that evoke? In contrast, the Chinese couple who actually used the various establishments were specific, unique individuals. 'Both were personable, charming, and quick to win the admiration and respect of those they had the opportunity to become intimate with.' It is dangerous to argue from the general to the particular. Many prejudiced individuals often protest that they can't in actual fact be prejudiced as some of their friends belong to the group in question. Very poor and very dangerous logic.

Of course all of the above criticisms also assume at the very least that the people responding to the questionnaire were the people who were actually in contact with the customers in the various establishments La Piere visited. But how often is a restaurant or motel owner or manager the one who waits on table or works on the reception? I suspect that the relationship between attitudes and behaviour is especially weak when it's one person's attitude and another person's behaviour that is assessed!

Overall, despite the fact that La Piere's study is very commonly cited in textbooks of social psychology, very few conclusions can be drawn from it. It did, however, provide an important stimulus to research on an important topic, and it is to the subsequent body of research that I now turn.

Reviews of the attitude–behaviour relationship

Although many theorists have been keen to push the idea that attitudes and behaviour are closely related, empirical studies have been very inconsistent in reporting such an association. An early literature review by Wicker (1969) concluded that there was a very poor overall relationship between attitudes and behaviours over a variety of issues. Rarely was more than 10 per cent of the variability in behaviour accounted for by the attitude assessment. Somewhat later, Hanson (1980) reviewed 46 studies and found that 18 out of 26 laboratory studies reported a positive relationship between attitudes and behaviour. In contrast, 16 out of 20 field studies failed to show such a relationship. It seems that in the more controlled conditions of the laboratory the relationship is more likely to be detected. These studies highlighted the fact that there is no simple attitude–behaviour relationship, and that other factors must be taken into consideration. Especially important may be situational constraints, and especially the conflicting attitudes these may evoke, and the way in which attitude and behavioural measurements are undertaken. In the next sections I will examine each of these in turn.

Attitude–behaviour specificity

One reason that research is inconsistent in showing a relationship between attitudes and behaviour is that the constructs are often measured at different levels of specificity (Ajzen and Fishbein, 1980). So, for example, the attitude assessed may be a general evaluation of a particular class of attitude objects (perhaps an ethnic group), whereas the behaviour assessed may be specific, towards a particular person who is a member of that group, or behaviour in a specific context or social situation. Behaviours are always specific and yet attitudes are often assessed at a very general level. Little surprise then that they often seem to be only weakly related. But there are additional factors that must be taken into account as they may also affect the relationship between a specific attitude and behaviour. It is to these personal and situational factors that I turn next.

Personal and situational constraints

The reviews that I have already mentioned of the attitude–behaviour relationship both emphasised that attitudes do not exist in grand isolation. Their expression is likely to be influenced by a variety of other factors. At the very least, we must acknowledge that attitudes exist within a system, so there are likely to be competing attitudes and hence alternative behaviours that may be expressed in a given situation. Take the La Piere study, for example. Perhaps the positive reception the oriental couple received at the various establishments they visited was a reflection of the weak link between attitudes and behaviour, or maybe it was just that a more dominant attitude in that face-to-face situation was to be polite and not make a fuss. If that was the dominant attitude then the behaviour of the staff was perfectly in accord with their dominant attitude at the time.

The notion of competing attitudes does also raise the issue of the effect of situational factors on the behavioural expression of attitudes. As was evident in my example, specific situations may be more likely to elicit one attitude rather than another, and may sometimes have a distinctly inhibiting effect on the behavioural expression of some attitudes.

Perhaps one of the reasons that Hanson (1980) reported a better relationship between attitudes and behaviour in laboratory studies than in field studies was because there are likely to be fewer competing attitudes or inhibiting situational factors in a psychological laboratory. These considerations show why many studies prefer to use behavioural *intentions* rather than actual behaviour when discussing the attitude–behaviour link. It is a behavioural measure that is less likely to be distorted by the myriad of accidental or incidental personal and situational factors that may come between a behavioural intention and its expression. I may well intend to buy the latest super-biological soap powder after seeing the persuasive advert, but lack of money, the fact that it is not stocked by the local shop, and lack of time to go shopping may all block but not invalidate my behavioural intention.

Moderating variables

A number of variables have been highlighted as potentially moderating the strength of the attitude–behaviour link. First, our direct experience of the attitude object. It has been argued that where attitudes have been acquired through direct experience they may show a stronger relationship to behaviour (Fazio and Zanna, 1981). For example, although we may have a favourable attitude towards a product after seeing an advertisement for it, actually buying the product may be more likely if we have tried it (Krishnan and Smith, 1998).

In similar vein, people are more likely to act on their attitudes when they have a vested interest in doing so (Crano, 1997). If your college announced that it would be introducing mid-term examinations on all courses there would undoubtedly be a general negative response from students. However, if it were announced that this would not take effect until next year, then it is highly likely that it would be the students who would still be at the college next year who would be most active in some form of action against the introduction of the exams.

One way in which these results can be explained is in terms of attitude accessibility (Fazio, 1989) – the ease with which we can recall attitudes from memory and apply the evaluations associated with the attitude object. If we feel strongly about an issue or have direct experience of an attitude object, it is likely to be more vivid and easily recalled, to affect our behaviour, and to lead us to pay close attention to any attempt at persuasion on that particular topic (Fabrigar et al., 1998). Unfortunately, highly accessible attitudes may sometimes be too readily recalled and lead to us overlooking changes in the attitude object and instead seeing what is familiar and expected (Fazio *et al.*, 2000). Interpersonal attitudes such as liking and attraction may be highly accessible and perhaps this is at least partly the reason why many couples complain that their partner doesn't notice them any more, or at least doesn't notice differences and changes.

Behaviour and attitude change

Having examined how our existing attitudes may predict and influence behaviour, it is now appropriate to consider the consequences of counter-attitudinal behaviour. This has been a major topic of interest of a broad set of cognitive theories collectively known as *cognitive consistency theories*. These approaches argue that we generally strive to maintain a balance or consistency between the various components of our attitude system and between our attitudes and behaviour. Where there is imbalance we may feel uncomfortable and stressed.

One particular approach, Cognitive Dissonance Theory, has had a major impact on our understanding of how we reconcile discrepancies between our attitudes and behaviour. In particular, it tries to explain how counter-attitudinal behaviour may actually result in a change in attitudes. This approach has produced a vast and complex research literature clarifying the nature of these processes and will be given detailed examination. In the remaining sections of this chapter I will examine the basic theory of cognitive dissonance, its criticisms, alternative theories and modern developments.

Cognitive Dissonance Theory

Cognitive Dissonance Theory was originally developed by Leon Festinger (1957). In Cognitive Dissonance Theory, the elements of our attitude system may be consonant, dissonant or irrelevant to each other. Two elements are said to be consonant when one follows from the other. Thus, if we support a national political party we may vote for them at general elections. Elements are said to be dissonant when one presupposes the opposite of the other. So, we may support a national political party, but perhaps we are also voting tactically and so vote for another party at the general election. In terms of the situation where elements are seen as irrelevant, it may well be that, although we support one of the national political parties, when it comes to local elections we vote for a candidate based solely on their personal qualities and past record, regardless of political allegiance. You may have noticed that in the above example I appeared to be talking about attitudes and behaviour. In fact, it is worth noting at this point that, although Festinger's original formulation related to the consonance or otherwise of *any* two cognitions, almost all the research on Cognitive Dissonance Theory has had the attitude towards behaviour as one of its elements.

Cognitive Dissonance Theory argues that when we behave in a way that is inconsistent with our attitudes we experience a cognitive conflict that is uncomfortable and stressful. The extent of this discomfort will be dependent on the relative number of consonant and dissonant cognitions and the importance of each of these for the person. For example, when you choose which modules to take as a part of your course, you may have to decide between one which is highly interesting but will not be as useful when you seek employment after graduating, and another which may be more boring and harder work, and which your friends will not be taking, but which will be well received by prospective employers. The alternatives may have varying numbers of positive and negative cognitions associated with them, and each of the cognitions may vary in importance for the individual. Whichever alternative you chose, you would experience dissonance. If, however, you could choose a module that had all the major positive aspects and none of the negative aspects of the other choices, then you would be likely to experience little or no dissonance. Perhaps a third module is interesting, has a reasonable workload, will be taken by your friends and has the potential to be useful in employment terms.

The main point of Cognitive Dissonance Theory is that dissonance is uncomfortable and so the individual is motivated to restore a state of consonance. Festinger suggested three main ways in which people can go about restoring the congruence between attitudes and behaviour. First, you can change one of the dissonant elements, the attitude or behaviour. It is often the case that it is easier to change our attitudes than our behaviour, and so in these circumstances we may well find that attitudes are changed to come into line with behaviour. Second, you may seek information that supports your actions and thus brings your attitude back into line with your behaviour. For example, car buyers often seem to pay more attention to the advertisements for the model they have bought after making the purchase than before. If they have had to make a hard choice then they may be gathering information to justify their purchase decision. Finally, we may reduce dissonance by simply downgrading the importance of the attitude. After all, the car is for general family use and is simply a means of getting from A to B. And if you can manage to convince yourself of that, then maybe you will feel less dissonance after buying the small hatchback rather than the sports car!

More recent research also suggests that there are a variety of indirect methods by which we can reduce cognitive dissonance, or at least take away the discomfort associated with it. Simply expressing the discomfort that is felt can reduce it (Pyszczynski *et al.*, 1993); we may want to focus on and accent other positive aspects of our self or our behaviour rather than dwell on the dissonant behaviour (Lydon and Zanna, 1990), or find pleasure and distraction elsewhere, such as in alcohol, food or sporting activity (Steele *et al.*, 1981).

Although Cognitive Dissonance Theory has been criticised as vague and untestable in places, it has prompted a great deal of research, perhaps more than any other simple theory in social psychology. It is to this body of research and to the subsequent revisions of the basic theory that I now turn.

The $20/$1 experiment

A very famous study by Festinger and Carlsmith (1959) will illustrate the basic phenomenon of cognitive dissonance and the style of early research in the area. Participants in this experiment were recruited for a laboratory study supposedly on the topic of 'Measures of performance'. Participants in the experiment were required to perform two extremely boring and trivial tasks, each for half an hour. One task consisted of putting twelve spools on to a tray, emptying the tray and then repeating the procedure until the half hour was up. The second task consisted of turning each of forty-eight square pegs on a board a quarter-turn clockwise and then another quarter-turn; again, this was repeated for the full half hour. Unknown to the participants, the real experiment only began after the hour of extremely boring tasks. The participants were informed that the experiment had actually been to research the effects of expectancy on task performance, but they had been in the control condition, where no prior expectations had been created. One-third of the subjects – a control condition against which to compare the results of the subjects in the experimental condition – then simply waited in the secretary's office for a few minutes before proceeding to the post-experiment interview.

The two-thirds of subjects in the experimental condition were informed that the experimenter's research assistant had not turned up, and they were offered an amount of money to briefly take on this role. Their job would be to lead the next subject (actually a confederate) to believe that the experiment was interesting and enjoyable. For doing this the subject was offered either a nominal fee of $1 or the rather substantial sum of $20. This does not sound much now, but by today's standards the $20 is about the equivalent of £60. Of course this was really a double bluff (quite something to consider in ethical terms!) and the real interest was not in the supposed new subject but rather in whether the level of financial reward for engaging in the counter-attitudinal behaviour (saying an experiment was enjoyable and interesting when they had found it boring and far from enjoyable) affected their own evaluations of the study.

After their participation, the subjects in all conditions were interviewed by another person, supposedly unconnected with the experiment that they had just been involved in, under the guise of a departmental review of the current research that it was supporting. Subjects were asked a number of questions concerning the research they had participated in, including the extent to which they had found their participation enjoyable and interesting.

So what was the point of the experimental manipulation? Basically, subjects from the control condition and those who had been paid a lot of money should not have experienced any dissonance effects. The subjects in the control condition had not misled the new subjects, and the subjects in the $20 condition had a rather substantial fee to justify their behaviour (incidentally, the subjects in the experimental conditions were subsequently asked to return their fee). The subjects in these conditions did indeed rate the study as boring. In contrast, the subjects receiving $1 had no such easy extrinsic justification or explanation for their counter-attitudinal behaviour, and so might be expected to experience a higher level of cognitive dissonance.

Subjects in the $1 condition did indeed report finding the experiment more enjoyable than their counterparts in the other conditions. The ability of induced counter-attitudinal behaviour to produce a change in attitudes has been replicated in a number of subsequent studies, although the explanation for such changes has aroused considerable theoretical controversy. From the wealth of subsequent research came both alternative theoretical explanations of the phenomenon and refinements of Cognitive Dissonance Theory itself.

The study of attitude change contingent upon induced compliance has many real-life parallels. What of the parents who pay their children to do their homework or perform well at school? If this is a relatively small reward for engaging in a task they find unpleasant, then it may well produce in them a more positive attitude to the subject in the long run. But their initial attitude to the task may be crucial. If they enjoy the task already, then rewarding them for undertaking it will not produce dissonance, but it may produce an over-justification effect; the children may attribute their behaviour to the rewards they have received and discount any intrinsic motivation or interest. No doubt the very opposite of the effect the parents intended!

In similar vein, dissonance theory may have important implications for the parent who wants to reduce undesirable behaviour in their child – for example, if a parent wishes a child to refrain from some activity. Perhaps the child uses items of equipment that the parent thinks are potentially dangerous and so the child is told not to use the equipment except under supervision. Does it make a difference whether the parent gently explains this prohibition or imposes severe threats and sanctions for non-compliance with the injunction? If you think about this in cognitive dissonance terms you will see that there are quite different potential consequences resulting from these different discipline strategies. The alternative scenarios may go something like this. Gently prohibited from using the equipment, the child has no explanation from the external environment for their compliance. So they have the conflict over the fact that they are complying and not doing something they wish to do for little apparent reason. They may thus change their attitude to one of not really being keen on that activity anyway. That will explain why they do not engage in it. In contrast, the parent issuing severe injunctions and penalties may indeed manage to gain compliance, but the child will have little reason to alter its attitude to the activity. The child can explain its behaviour quite rationally as simply a means of avoiding punishment. In the longer term, will the child always be able to resist the temptation of the activity? By and large, dissonance theory would seem to suggest that, in the long run, and where practical, control strategies that place the onus on the child will be more effective than those that impose control externally. The former may win hearts and minds; the latter may simply produce grudging and possibly only temporary compliance.

Revisions to basic dissonance theory

Since its launch, the original formulation of dissonance theory has evolved into a somewhat more complex form. In this section I will examine some of the major clarifications and refinements that have been made to the original theory.

The role of volition and commitment

Two early revisions to Cognitive Dissonance Theory were made by Brehm and Cohen (1962). They argued, and provided evidence through a series of empirical studies, that for dissonance to occur after making a decision the individual must perceive that they made that decision of their own free will (volition), and there must be an element of psychological commitment to the decision.

In terms of volition, we can well imagine that in the Festinger and Carlsmith study (see pp. 74–76) it is highly unlikely that any dissonance effects would have occurred had subjects simply been ordered to lie to the confederate subject about how much they had enjoyed the experiment. An interesting recent study also highlights some of the everyday implications of this factor. Many minority groups protest about jokes that they consider disparaging, and a frequent response is that such jokes are harmless. But dissonance theory suggests (and this is supported by empirical research) that if you freely choose to tell such jokes then maybe they will affect your attitude to the group in question and your attitude may become more negative (Hobden and Olson, 1994).

Commitment concerns the reversibility of a decision or action. When we make a choice between two products in a shop we are much less likely to experience dissonance if we know that we can return the product later if we change our mind and decide it is unsuitable. We often use public commitment to help us keep to our decisions. People often believe that they will find it easier to stick to New Year's resolutions, such as going on a diet or giving up smoking, if they have publicly announced their intentions. And there is some justification for this idea. For example, evidence suggests that the making public of pro-minority essays that white subjects have been induced to write may actually make the subjects' own attitudes towards the minority group more favourable, especially if there is an element of ambivalence in these attitudes in the first place (Leippe and Eisenstadt, 1994).

Self-esteem

Starting with Aronson (1968), a number of authors have stressed the significance of self-esteem for dissonance effects (e.g. Steele,

1988). The basic idea is that people with high self-esteem will regard themselves as having a relatively high level of control in their lives and consequently are able to maintain a relatively high level of cognitive consistency. Consequently, engaging in counter-attitudinal behaviour is likely to threaten this perception and create a feeling of dissonance. This should motivate the individual to use one of the mechanisms that I have already mentioned to reduce the dissonance, restore consonance and re-affirm their original beliefs about themselves and their competence (Prislin and Pool, 1996). The converse of this picture should also be true: individuals low in self-esteem probably expect that they will do inconsistent things and are not masters of their own fate. So counter-attitudinal behaviour does not have to be explained away; it is just another aspect of their low expectation and perception of themselves. They are less likely to experience dissonance when they engage in counter-attitudinal behaviour.

Self-Perception Theory

In reading the above account of Cognitive Dissonance Theory it may have struck you that, although the theory is concerned about cognitive structures and process, these are inferred, they are hypothetical constructs. It is a short step from this observation to the question as to whether we actually need to make these inferences in order to be able to explain the observed effects of counter-attitudinal behaviour. Certainly the advocates of the self-perception approach (Bem, 1968) would argue that such inferential leaps are not necessary. For many years this approach was a true thorn in the side of dissonance theory and it proved extremely difficult to design experiments to clearly favour one theory or the other.

You may recall Bem's basic approach to attitudes from Chapter 1. His basic argument is that people's attitude statements are at least in part a reflection of their observations of their own behaviour and the contexts in which it occurs – much in the same way that other people would infer our attitudes from observing our behaviour. There is some evidence that people can and do indeed observe their own behaviour and environmental contexts and use this as a basis for inferring attitudes and emotional states. Schachter and Singer's (1962) study is a very famous example of this. In conditions of unexplained physiological arousal, subjects looked to environmental cues and the behaviour of other individuals to explain and label their physical state. This has been called the *two-factor theory of emotion* – stressing that emotions have both biological and social elements. This idea has significant implications, some of which have been experimentally demonstrated. For example, this theory has been adapted to explain the nature of passionate love. Maybe we sometimes fall in love in times of perceived danger as a result of mis-attributing our heightened arousal to the presence of the other person (Hatfield and Rapson, 1996). Perhaps roller-coaster owners should promote their rides as the place to take your date if you want them to fall in love with you! Similarly, a phobic response may be reduced if the person can label their physiological arousal as resulting from some source other than the feared object, or if they can be helped to see their physiological reaction to the stimulus as lower than it actually is. Learning to re-attribute the causes of personal and behavioural problems may also be a significant part of much cognitive-behavioural therapy (e.g. Cheung, 1996).

In the context of cognitive dissonance experiments such as the $20/$1 experiment, when we observe ourselves praising the boring experimental experience to the next subject, and do not have a large amount of money or other external justification to explain that behaviour, maybe we infer that we did actually enjoy it to a certain degree. In a similar way, Self-Perception Theory can also explain the volition and commitment amendments to Cognitive Dissonance Theory. If we perceive we had no choice of action, and our behaviour does not imply an irrevocable commitment, then we do not need to change our existing attitude. The behaviour will be reflecting an altogether different attitude, towards money or choice.

Dissonance and physiological arousal

Although many ingenious and complex experiments attempted to distinguish the relative merits of Cognitive Dissonance Theory and

Self-Perception Theory, their results were largely inconclusive for many years. Eventually theorists suggested a way out of the stalemate – by treating Festinger's idea that dissonance engendered discomfort as implying that there was an element of physiological arousal involved in the process. This opened up new avenues for research. Is arousal necessary for cognitive dissonance effects to occur? If yes, this would support Cognitive Dissonance Theory. If no, this would support Self-Perception Theory.

In effect, the main theoretical difference between Self-Perception Theory and dissonance theory is that the latter proposes that there is some psychological discomfort and physiological arousal associated with behaving in a way counter to our attitudes. Research has largely confirmed that dissonance is associated with physiological arousal (Croyle and Cooper, 1983) and feelings of discomfort (Elliot and Devine, 1994). Drugs that increase or reduce arousal have also been shown to correspondingly increase or reduce dissonance effects (Cooper et al., 1978; Steele et al., 1981).

Of course we don't tend to agonise over every little counter-attitudinal decision, and so there may still be a place for Self-Perception Theory in explaining how behaviour may bring about attitude change in some situations. Where there is little personal investment or significance in the attitude it may be that we do not experience physiological arousal and discomfort over counter-attitudinal behaviour. I feel pretty sure that when I pick one apple over another in the supermarket I do not feel an awful lot of conflict over the decision. In these low-key situations we may simply observe our behaviour, make appropriate inferences and modify our attitudes accordingly. To a large extent it may be sensible to see Self-Perception Theory and Cognitive Dissonance Theory as complementary explanations of attitude change resulting from counter-attitudinal behaviours which may vary in their affective or emotional significance for the individual.

There is most definitely one area where Self-Perception Theory would seem to have the edge over dissonance theory: explaining over-justification effects. We have already mentioned this effect earlier in this chapter – it is the situation where an individual is rewarded for engaging in an already enjoyable activity. There is certainly no dissonance here. But individuals may perceive it as paradoxical that they are being rewarded for something they want to do anyway. One way to rationalise this paradox is for them to observe the context of their behaviour and revise their attitudes accordingly. Maybe they don't enjoy the activity as much as they initially thought. The result is a change to a more negative evaluation of the activity in question (Freedman *et al.*, 1992).

Summary

This chapter examined the relationship between attitudes and behaviour from two perspectives: first, the extent to which attitudes predict corresponding behaviours; and second, how counter-attitudinal behaviour can sometimes produce changes in attitudes. In terms of the attitude–behaviour link, the two appear most clearly related in the laboratory. In the real world a multitude of personal and situational factors may prevent attitudes from being reflected in behaviour. The attitude–behaviour link is also clearer if we examine specific attitudes towards specific behaviours, and attitudes that are highly accessible in the person's memory – that is, based on experience and with personal significance for the individual. In terms of attitude change resulting from counter-attitudinal behaviour, there is an extensive literature supporting a cognitive dissonance explanation, although this explanation has itself been much refined since it was first proposed. The alternative approach of Self-Perception Theory is considerably more limited in this domain, although it has important implications in its explanation of over-justification effects that may reduce the positive attitude to enjoyable tasks when they are rewarded.

Further reading

Breckler, S. J. (1984) Empirical validation of affect, behavior and cognition as distinct components of attitude. *Journal of Personality and*

Social Psychology, 47, 1191–1205. Despite the central position of the triadic model of attitudes within the field, the notion has received little systematic research attention. This is one of the main validating studies to date.

Fazio, R. H. and Williams, C. J. (1986) Attitude accessibility as a moderator of the attitude-perception and attitude-behavior relations: an investigation of the 1984 presidential election. *Journal of Personality and Social Psychology*, 51, 505–514. A real-life illustration of how higher levels of attitude accessibility are associated with selective attention to confirmatory information and greater attitude–behaviour consistency.

La Piere, R. T. (1934) Attitudes vs. actions. *Social Forces*, 13, 230–237. A classic much-cited article from the early days of the attitude–behaviour debate.

Chapter 5

Changing attitudes

Introduction

PEOPLE HAVE BEEN INTERESTED in the factors that make arguments persuasive since long before psychology was established as a separate discipline. The art of persuasive speaking was the subject of considerable study in ancient Greece, and the Greek philosophers such as Plato devoted much effort to understanding the principles that made messages persuasive. Whether it is based on philosophical analysis or simply wanting to sway an audience in public speaking, the art of persuasion is truly ancient. The relatively recent contribution of psychology has been to turn the philosophical analysis and the art of persuasion into a subject for scientific investigation. In this chapter I will examine some of the major factors that have been shown to influence the effectiveness of a persuasive communication.

Communication has been defined as 'who says what to whom with what effect' (Smith *et al.*, 1946). Persuasive communication, no less than other forms of communication, needs to consider these various aspects. The effects component has been partially dealt with in our consideration of the relationship between attitudes and behaviour; it will be given further consideration in Chapter 6 when I consider two psychological theories of the persuasive process. The other factors – the who says what to whom – will be considered in this chapter. I will follow the common practice of calling the originator of the persuasive message the source, and the person or people it is directed at the audience. What is said is, of course, the message. To give a rounded treatment of these subjects, I will also consider the medium of communication as a factor in persuasion. Given the diversity of the modern media, their impact can vary considerably.

Although I will be examining source, message, audience and media factors separately, it is important to remember that they may in fact interact and either enhance or reduce each other's impact. For example, a highly persuasive message may be less so if we become aware of the vested interests of the communicator. Similarly, a message that is highly persuasive to one group of intelligent recipients may fail miserably with another group of less intelligent individuals because it is too complex for them to understand.

Not only may the source, message and audience factors enhance or reduce the effectiveness of a persuasive message, but it is important to remember that they may affect the perception of each other, and that a persuasive message may affect the perception of these factors in persuasion. For example, what an audience thinks of a communicator may be influenced by what they think of his or her message. This is evident in the similarity attraction effects that are so frequently noted by social psychologists. An advertisement espousing similar attitudes to your own, perhaps from a political party, will not only be likely to persuade you of the truth of its message but will also make you like the political party more. This shows the interrelatedness of source and message factors. In similar vein, we often see attractive models used in advertisements on the basis that they will be more persuasive, but there is also evidence that we tend to see people who we agree with as more attractive! The bottom line is that there are often complex patterns of reciprocal influence among the persuasive factors and effects that I will be examining. I will highlight some of these interconnections as we go along, but there are many more than we will have time to cover here.

Message learning

An early attempt to represent the link between source, message and audience effects examined the extent to which they promoted or inhibited the learning and acceptance of the persuasive communication (McGuire, 1968). It is important to note that from this perspective a persuasive communication may simultaneously both facilitate and inhibit attitude change. For example, a fear appeal may reduce attention and hence the ability to learn a message and yet increase the likelihood of accepting the message if it is learned.

Although two major processes have been identified in terms of the impact of a persuasive communication – learning (attention to and comprehension of the message) and acceptance or yielding – these can be broken down into a series of five sequential steps that are necessary for attitude change (persuasion) to be seen to occur:

1   Attention to the message
2   Comprehension of the message
3   Yielding to (acceptance of) the message
4   Retention of the message in memory
5   Acting as a result

Although a great deal of research has focused on the acceptance stage, all are important, and we will see in the remainder of this chapter how they may be affected by the characteristics of the source message, audience and medium of communication. Although the message learning approach has to a large extent been superseded by more sophisticated theoretical analyses, it is a useful approach for organising our review of the factors involved in persuasion.

Source

Messages can be delivered by sources at different levels of abstraction. If I am trying to persuade you to buy a charity lottery ticket then we could analyse my effectiveness as a source. When we read a newspaper we may regard that as a source of persuasive communication; when we see an advertisement from a charity we may regard the charity as a source. In short, a source may be a person, group or institution. But why should the different sources of persuasive messages be more or less effective? Quite simply, in identifying the source of a persuasive communication we have additional information to that contained in the message. A message arguing against the death penalty is likely to be received very differently if we are led to believe that it was made by a convict on death row rather than by a prosecution lawyer. Their very evident different self-interests would undoubtedly colour our interpretation of the intent of the persuasive communication.

Types of source effect

Two main types of source effect have been investigated: attractiveness and credibility. Research into the role of attractiveness has examined both physical attractiveness and the likeability of the source. Studies of credibility have examined both expertise and trustworthiness, although these were not clearly separated in some early studies.

To a very great degree, how we evaluate a source is a matter of personal judgement or *attribution*. One person may like an actor or actress and find them attractive; another may actually be repulsed by them. These attributions may sometimes be made on the basis of totally irrelevant information, such as race, sex, and physical appearance. The police or government experts may be considered credible by some individuals and as very far from objective and credible by others. That was certainly very evident in the perceptions of experts both in this country and in France and Germany during the crisis over BSE ('mad cow disease') in British cattle, and in the dispute over whether beef was safe to eat. Regardless of whether or not the experts were biased, a high level of personal involvement can make for very biased attributions of their expertise and trustworthiness.

Studying source effects

The typical format for much of the foundation research in this area was quite straightforward. Typically subjects would have their attitudes assessed on some topic of interest. Then, some time later, half of them would be presented with a persuasive communication, perhaps presented as a newspaper article. Those not presented with a persuasive communication would function as a control group to provide a baseline for the amount of attitude change that may occur naturally, without being subject to the persuasive communication. Those subjects receiving the persuasive communication – the experimental group – may be told that it comes from either a high-status source, such as a reputable, 'serious' newspaper, or else a low-reputation tabloid. After the persuasive attempt, all the subjects – those in the control group and the experimental group – again complete an attitude questionnaire to assess the extent of their change in attitude, if any, on the crucial topics. By comparing the differences between the groups we can determine if identifying the source had any effect in comparison to the baseline, and whether different types of source had different types or magnitudes of effect. As the only difference between the groups was the identification of the source, any differences in attitude change can only be attributed to the characteristics of the source.

In the above discussion of the method by which source effects are often studied I left out one significant piece of information: when the source is identified. Should the source be identified at the beginning or end of a persuasive communication or advertisement? If you ponder this for a moment you will appreciate its potential significance. Initial revelation might distract attention *or* promote attention and learning of the message.

An experiment by Mills and Harvey (1972) will illustrate this point. Subjects read a passage in favour of a broader education for college students, which was attributed to sources varying in their expertise and attractiveness. The subjects were told about the source either at the beginning or at the end of the message. For expert sources, persuasion was greater if the expert was identified at the start of the message. But for the attractive sources, persuasiveness was not affected by whether the source was revealed at the start or the end of the message. This suggested the possibility that expertise may affect how a recipient thinks about a message, while source attractiveness does not; maybe it has a direct impact in its own right. A good omen for the advertisers!

Credibility

Hovland and Weiss (1951) were the first researchers to systematically test for persuasion effects due to source factors. A group of subjects were given a questionnaire on four critical topics (antihistamines remaining prescribed drugs; the possibility of developing an atomic submarine; industry's responsibility for the steel shortage; the decline of cinema being due to TV). Remember this experiment was conducted in the late 1940s, hence the topics may seem rather dated now, but they were controversial at the time. One week later the subjects were given four newspaper articles (including one in favour of or against one of the test issues). Some of the articles were attributed to high-credibility sources and others to low-credibility sources. For example, in the case of the antihistamines this might have been a medical journal or a mass circulation newspaper. The subjects were then given the second questionnaire.

Comparison of the pre-/post-questionnaire determined the attitude-change effects of the communication and also contained questions on the factual content of the communications to confirm that any differences did not result from differences in levels of attention to the message. On average the high-credibility sources produced a 22.5 per cent change in attitudes, the low-credibility sources a mere 8.4 per cent. This pattern of results might be expected, but perhaps more interesting was the finding of a sleeper effect – an increase in persuasion from the low-credibility source over time: After four weeks the impact of the sources was equal. Over time it seems that informational content may become more important than the source of the message. However, more recent research has suggested that sleeper effects do only tend to occur under very specific, limited conditions.

Greenwald *et al.* (1986) suggest that the sleeper effect occurs because the message and the information about the low-credibility source or counter-argument (the discounting cue) decay at different rates. Thus the initial impact of the low-credibility source decreases over time and the message comes to have a relatively greater impact. In order for a sleeper effect to occur, the differential decay hypothesis argues that some important requirements must be met. First, the persuasive message must have a strong initial impact on the recipient. If the subject has not learned the persuasive message initially then there is no chance it can gain in significance later. To ensure the message is learned, some experimenters may require the subject to make notes on the arguments. Second, the discounting cue (that the communication is untrustworthy) must be presented immediately *after* the message and effectively oppose the impact of the message. This is to ensure that subjects do not 'switch off' their attention to the message, and it also prevents possible changes in the way the message is cognitively processed and stored in memory. Finally, the discounting cue must decay more rapidly than the message. The end result is that the message effect, even though it is itself decaying, appears more strongly after a period of time has elapsed than it did while suppressed by the influence of the discounting cue.

The nature of credibility

The significance of credibility in persuasion may be affected by two main factors: the person's level of interest in the area of concern, and the perceived intentions of the communicator.

In terms of the person's level of interest, credibility is most likely to be influential if they have relatively little interest or involvement in the persuasive issue – in other words, if they are likely to accept the other person's opinion with relatively little thought or criticism. If an issue has personal significance for us then this is not likely to be the case. We will have prior knowledge and be highly motivated to examine any persuasive communication that attacks an existing important attitude. In these circumstances a high-credibility source may actually increase the thought given to a message and persuasion may be less likely (Petty *et al.*, 1981). Unfortunately, laboratory studies are typically on unimportant issues and use high-credibility sources. Little wonder that they often report such powerful credibility effects on persuasion.

The perceived intentions of the communicator play a crucial role in determining whether we trust them. This is an attributional issue that I briefly mentioned at the start of this chapter. The trust that we attribute to the source is likely to be greatest when we perceive them as arguing against their own self-interest and with nothing personal to gain, and possibly even losing out through persuading us.

This may explain the power of advertisements using ordinary shoppers approached without warning to give their views on a product. Unlike the paid professional actors, we do not see these ordinary shoppers as having any ulterior motive or vested interest in persuading us, and hence they are inherently more trustworthy.

Attractiveness

The attractiveness of a communicator has been shown to be a very major factor in their persuasiveness. Two aspects of attractiveness have received a considerable amount of attention: the impact of physical appearance, and the likeability of the communicator.

Research generally suggests a simple linear relationship between the physical attractiveness of the communicator and persuasion (Patzer, 1985), although this may in part be reflecting other correlating characteristics such as the self-esteem or communication skills of more attractive individuals (Chaiken, 1979).

It also suggests that people are more persuaded by communicators who are perceived as similar and liked (Eagly and Chaiken, 1975). Similarity is usually found to be associated with liking. Building on this implication of similarity, it has been found that if a source initially expresses some views held by his audience then a subsequent persuasion attempt is likely to be more successful. This strategy has been termed 'beating the dead horse' (Cialdini, 1993).

Explaining source effects

Some theorists have stressed attributional explanations for many of the source effects that have been noted as factors. Because we trust someone or believe them to be an expert, and so objective in their views, we may effectively take a short cut through the persuasion process and miss out the element of comprehension (Chaiken, 1987) – essentially taking the expert's or trusted individual's word as truth about the attitude object. A study by Wood and Eagly (1981) looked at recipients' attributions, comprehension and attitude change in response to a persuasive communication. As one might expect, greater comprehension generally led to increased persuasion. Showing the impact of attributional factors, persuasion was also greater when the expected position of the communicator was violated and when the communicator appeared to be arguing against their own best interest. This perception of the communicator as unbiased, as influenced by the persuasive arguments rather than self-interest, was also associated with lower levels of comprehension, showing less attention by subjects to the message arguments and a consequent shortening of the persuasion process.

The attributional approach has been criticised as having limited applicability because people will often have limited information on which to base attributions (Cialdini and Petty, 1981). Having said this, people often do make attributions in the real world when they have limited information. They do this by drawing on memories, making assumptions and generalising from similar situations.

Other theorists stress the cognitive processing of persuasive information to explain source effects on persuasion. If high-credibility sources produce less thinking about a communication, then this may produce higher or lower levels of persuasion, depending on the nature of the persuasive message. In counter-attitudinal instances the short-circuiting may indeed produce more change than if a person seriously considers the issues involved. But in the situation where the person already favours the attitudinal stance in the persuasive message, not giving attention to and thinking about the content of the message may result in *less* persuasion than would have been the case with a less distracting source. The cognitive response approach to persuasion is discussed in detail in Chapter 6.

Message

Research has examined the impact of both rational persuasive messages and emotional appeals. This section will focus on one area that has received a particularly large amount of attention, the use of fear in persuasive appeals. This is very common in health advertising and public health campaigns. Before embarking on that topic it is appropriate to consider as a foundation the findings of the early research on the impact of some simple message characteristics on persuasion. A considerable number of message characteristics have been examined to ascertain their impact on persuasion. In this section I will examine some of the major findings.

Comprehension, number and order of arguments

As one might expect, message comprehensibility is a fairly fundamental prerequisite for an effective persuasive message. The more comprehensible a message, the more recall there is of its arguments and the higher the level of persuasion is likely to be (Eagly, 1974). At a very basic level, it would be difficult to be persuaded by an argument you don't understand. The number of arguments in a persuasive message is also likely to be important (Calder *et al.*, 1974). The greater the number of persuasive arguments that are presented, the greater the level of persuasion that is likely – within limits. It is, of course, possible to make arguments too long-winded and lose your audience's attention, or make the argument difficult to comprehend. And basic memory research does warn us that that we may find it difficult to remember a large number of arguments.

The order in which arguments are presented in a persuasive message may be especially important in situations where the target audience is going to receive opposing communications on a topic. For example, should a politician speak first or last in a debate, to have maximum impact? Do you want your advertisement at the front of the magazine, before all the others, or at the back, after them? The effectiveness of the persuasive appeal – and hence winning an election or having an effective advert that boosts sales – could depend on this decision. Unfortunately there is no easy answer to which is best. A lot seems to rest on the timing of the two communications and the opportunity this gives for the forgetting of either or both messages (Miller and Campbell, 1959). In general, if the two messages are presented at the same time but there is a time lapse before the attitude is assessed or a decision is made, this seems to favour the first message – a *primacy effect*. If there is a time delay after the first message but the impact of the messages is assessed immediately after the second, this seems to favour the acceptance of the second message – a *recency effect*. If both messages are presented at the same time and there is no delay in assessment, or if there is an equal delay after each message and before the assessment, then neither seems to be advantaged.

One- and two-sided messages

The issue of whether to present a one- or two-sided persuasive message has been given considerable attention by advertisers, politicians and propagandists in general. On the one hand, a two-sided message may appear more open and honest. On the other hand, do we want the person to realise that there is an alternative way of looking at the issues of concern? In part, the issue of whether to use one- or two-sided messages may depend on your target audience (Hovland *et al.*, 1949). If they are sympathetic to your cause, then a one-sided appeal may well be very effective.

But if they are unsympathetic that approach may be interpreted as underhand and deceitful. An unsympathetic audience may already know many of the counter-arguments to your persuasive appeal, so what harm is there in repeating them – and refuting them? This will also make the persuasive message appear more honest and trustworthy.

A potentially important consequence to the propagandist is the *inoculation effect* that a two-sided message may produce (Lumsdaine and Janis, 1953). With a one-sided message it may well be that, even though we persuade you to our cause now, in the long term someone else will come along and persuade you that you are mistaken and that the opposite is true. One possible way around this future threat to our persuasive plans is to present you with the counter-arguments in advance (with arguments against their acceptance), so that when they are encountered in real life you are forearmed and better able to resist the counter-persuasion. This is the inoculation effect. Sneaky, but a useful tool for the propagandist! Inoculation effects have a number of important practical uses in the real world. A number of studies, for example, have shown that it can be effective in life skills programmes which aim to persuade adolescents not to take up smoking and to help them resist peer pressures to smoke (Pfau et al., 1992).

To draw or not to draw conclusions?

In deciding whether to make the conclusions of a persuasive argument explicit, the propagandist must consider the extent to which the audience can be relied on to do it for themselves. If you can be fairly sure that the audience will draw the conclusions for themselves, then it may be best to let them do so. Information in the form of inferences they provide themselves is likely to be more trusted than any provided by an outside source. But if the audience is not likely to draw the crucial conclusion we go right back to the issue of comprehension; they will not have the full argument and so will be less persuaded. It seems that the issue of whether or not to draw explicit conclusions in a persuasive communication comes down quite simply to a judgement of the ability (which may include intelligence) and motivation of the target audience to deal with the persuasive message (McGuire, 1968).

Confidence

This topic has been investigated by a number of studies using simulated jury trial. Hesitancy about your message is not persuasive! In general, a message presented in a more confident, powerful style is more likely to be accepted (Bradac *et al.*, 1981). Lawyers, who regularly argue that not only is their client innocent but that the evidence makes that fact patently obvious, have long known this. After all, if your own lawyer, who knows you and the evidence well, can't be confident about your innocence, then how can a jury be expected to be convinced of the argument? This style of speaking may also give the speaker an air of credibility and achieve its effects at least in part through that factor, although research suggests that it may be important to take gender into account. While a powerful style of speech (low in hesitancies, qualifying statements, etc.) seems to almost universally advantage male speakers, it may be more complicated for female speakers and depend on the gender of the recipient. Carli (1990) found that a powerful speech style tended to reduce a speaker's credibility with male recipients but increased credibility with female recipients. Gender role stereotyping may be a crucial factor in this effect, but it is also likely that the specific situation (work or social) and the perceived goals of the communicator (e.g. are they trying to sell you something?) will also be taken into account in the real world.

Fear

There has been a large amount of research on message effects looking at the effects of fear arousal. Fear has been defined in terms of an emotional response and in terms of message content (see Boster and Mongeau, 1984). Early approaches to the use of fear in persuasion examined it as a *drive* state. Fear increased an aversive drive state, and attitude change served to reduce that state. In addition, higher levels of fear should make people easier to condition and make them less able to produce complex, novel counter-arguments against a persuasive message.

The conclusion drawn from early research was that fear appeals may produce two basic needs in the individual: emotional and cognitive (Leventhal, 1970). The emotional need is to deal with the immediate fear arousal itself. The second need is to deal with the danger that produced the heightened fear arousal. Two ways of satisfying these needs are possible. A relatively maladaptive approach would be simply to deny the danger referred to in the message. So a smoker may say that the actual chances they will get lung cancer are minimal, as they know lots of people who have smoked all their life and are healthy, they are young and will give up in later life, they do not inhale (yes, I have heard that one!), they are only social smokers and do not smoke very many cigarettes, and so on. In contrast, they may cope with the fear by dealing with the danger directly. So maybe the smoker will actually try to give up smoking, heavy drinkers will try to drink less, couples may practise safe sex, injecting drug users may not share syringes and so on. So what makes the difference? What makes one person adopt the relatively adaptive way of coping with a fear message, and another choose the less adaptive way?

We can at least help the target audience to choose the adaptive coping strategy rather than denial by making that choice easier. The fewer obstacles and inconveniences to adopting the adaptive response, the more likely it is to be adopted (Zhang et al., 1999). An effective fear appeal may make specific recommendations for coping behaviour and provide necessary information and other resources. So, if we want to encourage sexually active young people to engage in safe sex, it will help if we inform them what safe practices are, tell them where they can obtain condoms, have sources of supply and information in convenient locations, remove any sources of embarrassment, and ensure there are few or no costs involved.

Subjective Expected Utility models

Subjective Expected Utility (SEU) models present clear and testable theoretical ideas about the nature of fear effects. SEU is the extent to which a choice or action has subjective value or utility for the individual, and the subjective probability that the choice or action will produce that outcome. Note that this utility is subjective, it is in the eye of the beholder. One action or decision does not implicitly have greater utility than another. So the argument goes that when people are faced with decisions, such as when they are given a choice of behaviours with different outcomes attached, they will choose the one with the greatest SEU for them. In practical terms this is often translated as the value or desirability of an outcome for the individual multiplied by its probability. If you are a smoker you can probably assign a value to the various outcomes of smoking – such as coughing, the likelihood of cancer, the enjoyment of the activity, etc. – but you can probably also weight these outcomes according to how likely you think each of these consequences is for you. Because the emphasis in this approach is on the individual's perception of risk and protection, any factors that affect these perceptions are also important. These perceptions may potentially be influenced by a variety of indirect factors such as age, gender and ethnicity.

Rogers's Protection Motivation Theory was an early example of an SEU model applied to fear appeals. Rogers (1975) argued that fear appeals depended on three aspects of perception: the perceived noxiousness of the threat, the perceived susceptibility to the threat, and the perceived efficacy of the possible coping response. In a later addition to his theory Rogers (1983) also emphasised the role of self-efficacy – a person's belief in their own ability to effectively execute the required coping response. In simple terms, an effective fear appeal would be likely to convince you that the threat is significant and highly likely to happen to you personally but that there is an effective way of avoiding it. Finally, you must believe that you have the ability to implement this effective solution if you are to accept the message (Witte, 1992). If any of these factors are discounted, the appeal is likely to fail. If we see the danger as minor we may ignore it. Similarly, if we see the danger as not applying to us we may ignore it. This may explain why fear appeals are more successful with older people rather than adolescents who see themselves as relatively invulnerable (Boster and Mongeau, 1984).

In terms of the perceived efficacy of the coping response, this would be evaluated on a cost versus benefit basis. Costs may be actual financial implications, inconvenience and time constraints. Benefits may be positive or negative; it could be a gain in health or some pleasure forgone. For example, AIDS studies have shown that many adolescents believe in the benefits of condom use but also believe that they reduce the pleasure of sexual intercourse. These negative perceptions are associated with lower condom usage (Valdiserri et al., 1989).

Audience

The characteristics of the target audience are undoubtedly a major factor in the effectiveness of a persuasive communication, but this is also a very fragmented area with a considerable number of factors that may be implicated. Many of these factors overlap with areas already covered earlier in this chapter. For example, the effects of many source or message characteristics may depend on the characteristics of the audience. A number of these interactions will be discussed in the course of this section.

Intelligence and self-esteem

The intelligence of a recipient will affect the number and complexity of arguments that can be handled within a message (Eagly and Warren, 1976).

Intelligence and self-esteem have both been implicated in affecting the balance between reception of (attention and comprehension of a message) and yielding to (actually being persuaded and retaining the message in memory) a persuasive communication. With higher levels of intelligence and self-esteem, recipients are more likely to attend to and understand the messages attempting to persuade them. But they are also more likely to question and resist persuasion attempts. The overall effect may be that increasing levels of intelligence and self-esteem are associated with greater levels of persuasion up to a certain point, because of their impact on the reception factor, but after that point persuasion may show a decline because of increasing scepticism and resistance to yielding.

Psychological reactance

Part of the explanation for people counter-arguing against persuasive messages in conditions where they have a particular interest and high level of personal involvement may be due to a phenomenon known as psychological reactance. In their theory of psychological reactance, Brehm and Brehm (1981) argue that people are generally motivated to retain their perceived freedom of choice and action. Thus if an individual believes that they have little choice or real say on an issue, or that their persuasion is taken as a foregone conclusion by the communicator, especially on an issue of importance to them, they may assert their independence by resisting the persuasion. Under these conditions people are likely to carefully examine a message and form counter-arguments; they may express a contrary view and behave in a contrary way to that sought.

This is illustrated in a study by Petty and Cacioppo (1977). This study showed that forewarning subjects about the persuasive intent of a future message (advocating that first- and second-year students be required to live in university accommodation) resulted in more topic-relevant thinking about the issue, and this in turn was associated with lower levels of persuasion. A similar effect was obtained by simply having subjects who were not forewarned write down their thoughts about the persuasive issue. It seems that simply giving thought to an important issue will activate the counter-arguments, with or without the forewarning of the persuasive intent.

Initial attitudes

Social judgement theory (Sherif and Hovland, 1961) argues that the likelihood of us accepting a persuasive message depends on whether it falls within our *latitude of acceptance* (openness to persuasion) or *latitude of rejection* (too distant from our initial attitude to be assimilated). Our latitude of acceptance is likely to be greater for attitudes that are relatively unimportant to us. Our latitude of rejection is likely to be greater if we hold extreme attitudes and for attitudes that have personal importance to us. For example, a study by Brown (1999) found that people were generally in favour of treatment as well as punishment for sex offenders, but they were considerably less supportive of this treatment being in their community. Where an attitude falls within our latitude of acceptance it is assimilated; where it fall outside of that area, in the latitude of rejection, it will tend to be contrasted. In other words, if a persuasive message is not accepted we may actually accentuate the difference between it and our existing attitude. If a political party attempts to persuade you of its message and fails, it may actually make you even more sure of your existing political preference and you may perceive the party as even less attractive than you did previously.

Sex differences

Many reviews and empirical studies have suggested that females are more easily persuaded than men. Eagly (1978) noted that this tended to be explained on the basis that women were more verbal than men, although studies of comprehension do not show this sex difference. Instead, Eagly argued that the apparent sex difference might reflect two factors. First, it may reflect the social role of women. This may explain the decline in the number of studies reporting a sex difference since the 1970s. Second, the sex differences may partly reflect an experimental artefact. The messages used in many studies of persuasion may be intrinsically more interesting to men than women. Hence they may be better informed about some of the topics, have more personal involvement and be more inclined to defend an existing attitude. In support of this assertion, Eagly conducted a content analysis of previous studies and found that those reporting a sex difference had indeed used topics that were rated as having more potential interest to males than females.

Medium

A number of important factors associated with how persuasive messages are communicated need to be considered to give a balanced account of the factors involved in persuasion. In this section I will consider the characteristics of the various modes of communication and the functions they may serve for the individual.

Media and channels of communication

Channel of communication refers to the mode of transmission of the message – for example, visual or auditory. Information may, of course, be communicated on more than one level, and information may be communicated unintentionally and in addition to any intended communication.

The channels involved in a persuasive communication will be determined by the medium through which the message is conveyed. At the simplest level this is face-to-face speech, but it also includes all the mass media in their various forms. The media of communication vary in the extent to which they emphasise language or non-verbal characteristics in a communication. The print media emphasise language; radio emphasises the language element of speech, although some non-linguistic speech characteristics are also communicated; and television programmes and advertisements operate on many verbal and non-verbal levels simultaneously. Little surprise that writers such as Marshall McLuhan (1964) argue that the nature of the medium itself may be as important as the message it carries in determining the way we think and behave.

The channels of communication vary in a number of characteristics that may affect the impact of a communicative message.

The different channels may vary in the senses they target – for example, visual or auditory; they may be more or less successful in actually reaching the targeted channels; they vary in the extent to which they are interactive with the audience, their permanence, and the extent to which they can be ignored. A newspaper primarily targets the visual system; its messages are primarily conveyed through language (although some of their pictures can be very powerful); the level of interaction with their audience is rather restricted, although it is possible to write or phone to give feed-back and comment. Newspapers are relatively permanent – the information can be consumed at the reader's own pace and you can always re-expose yourself to a message of interest – but the audience also selects whether to expose itself at all. Most people have their favourite newspaper and often focus on or read only certain sections of the newspaper. Similar pen portraits could be made for any medium of communication and highlight their potential strengths and limitations as tools for persuasive communications.

To maximise message effectiveness, the channel chosen for a persuasive communication must be given careful consideration. The choice of channel may depend on the characteristics of the source, message and audience. A complex message for a small specialist audience may be best presented through a specialist magazine. In contrast, a household product competing with many other similar products may use humour, music or attractive and well-known sources in a television advertisement. For maximum effectiveness, persuasive messages can be tailored to make best use of the characteristics of the channel(s) through which they are to be transmitted.

Media functions

People are not passive recipients of a message; they may use and selectively expose themselves to the various media to satisfy their individual needs and desires. This has been termed the uses and gratifications paradigm (Rubin, 1994). Because the various media may serve very different functions for different individuals, this has to be a factor when considering the mode of presentation for a persuasive message. For example, Lull (1980) highlights six functions that television may serve for the individual. We may use it for company, to regulate our behaviour, to promote communication, to learn how to act, to confirm competence, or to facilitate being with or avoiding other people. A message is more likely to get attention if the recipient perceives it as serving some function important to them. Lonely people may find escapism in the media (Perse and Rubin, 1990), while for others it may provide an instrumental function such as providing material for their social conversations (Perse, 1990). How often have we watched a television programme knowing that as likely as not we will be discussing it with our friends the next day?

Comparing channels

Personal communication is usually found to be the most powerful form of persuasion (e.g. Katz and Lazarsfeld, 1955). It is quite difficult to avoid a personal communication – you can't switch off a friend as easily as you can the television – and the message can be presented flexibly to accommodate any resistance or counter-arguments that may be raised.

Research confirms that the media vary in their effectiveness for communicating different types and complexity of persuasive message (Chaiken and Eagly, 1976). In general, complex messages appear to be most successful when presented in print rather than in the audio-visual media. Print allows the reader to take their time over a message, to think about it carefully and to re-read it if necessary – although these characteristics may also explain why messages in the printed media also tend to be received more critically than those in the audio-visual media. The audio-visual media provide their audience with much more information through several channels simultaneously. There are also many potential distractions from the message content. Thus these media may be best for relatively simple messages. Complex messages may be experienced as frustrating and unpleasant. The audio-visual media may be very effective persuaders, provided the message is comprehended; yielding may be greater than for the print media.

Summary

This chapter examined the major factors in persuasion: the source, message, audience and medium of a persuasive communication. In terms of source, I examined the effects of communicator credibility and attractiveness. The most obvious component of a persuasive communication is the message itself. The structure, content and organisation of the message may be crucial in determining its impact. The characteristics of the target audience, such as intelligence, self-esteem and existing attitude, may interact with both the source and message factors. Finally in this chapter, I looked at the effects of the medium of communication on the effectiveness of a persuasive message. This is an important aspect of persuasion but one that has received relatively little research attention from psychologists. The overall conclusion is that these factors are all interrelated, and for an effective persuasive communication all must be taken into account.

Further reading

Bryant, J. and Zillmann, D. (eds) (1994) *Media effects: advances in theory and research*. Hillsdale, NJ: Erlbaum. An interesting attempt to place persuasion in a broader context of media effects. A useful complement to more focused psychological accounts.

Shavitt, S. and Brock, T. C. (eds) (1994) *Persuasion: psychological insights and perspectives*. Boston, MA: Allyn & Bacon. A very readable book with a number of very relevant chapters by leading researchers.

Stiff, J. B. (1994) *Persuasive communication*. New York: Guilford Press. If you are only going to read one follow-up text, this is the one to go for. A readable, detailed, systematic account of theory and research on persuasion.

Chapter 6

Contemporary theories of persuasion

Introduction

IN THIS CHAPTER I WILL examine two of the major theoretical explanations of attitudes and persuasion. First, Ajzen and
Fishbein's (1980) Theory of Reasoned Action. As I have already
outlined a subjective expected utility model for health-related attitudes, this general approach should appear familiar. It may be
seen as having its roots in the behavioural tradition and arose
partly out of the general dissatisfaction with the classical triadic
model of attitudes. The second approach that I will examine is
the Elaboration Likelihood Model of persuasion (Petty and
Cacioppo, 1981; Petty and Wegener, 1999). This information-
processing model may be seen as having its roots firmly in the
cognitive tradition of attitude theory. Each theory has its advan-

tages, and they do differ in precisely what they are aiming to achieve. Ajzen and Fishbein present a general theory of attitudes, and place the evaluative dimension firmly at the centre of their theorising. Because this model is so clearly specified, research studies have been able to examine the impact of a variety of components on the persuasion and attitude-change process. As the title of their theory suggests, Ajzen and Fishbein are concerned primarily with the intended actions that are associated with attitudes. In contrast, the Elaboration Likelihood Model focuses directly on the cognitive effects of persuasive communications and arose out of a concern that previous research was actually examining two distinct types of persuasion. One was indeed rational and involved a great deal of message processing on the part of the recipient, but the other was less direct and based on a variety of cues such as physical appearance and status. This heuristic approach avoids the effort involved in the processing of large amounts of information, in favour of a more simple and direct accept or reject decision.

Ajzen and Fishbein's Theory of Reasoned Action

This theory appears commonsensical but it can be presented in a mathematical form and composed in such a way that it facilitates the measurement of its components. This leads to a big advantage for its scientific standing: it is potentially falsifiable. The fundamental equations proposed by the model to a large extent enable us to dissect the components of an individual's attitude. Not only can an attitude be assessed, but the significance of the attitude can also be established, and the components that give the attitude its significance can also be revealed. The implication of this is that the model acknowledges that attitude change may be achieved in a variety of ways; a number of components may be significant. This will become clear in an example that will be given after the model has been outlined in more detail.

Ajzen and Fishbein's model is often criticised as being too simplistic because it contains only two main factors (though they are subdivided): attitudes and subjective norms. These two components may be weighted differently in different situations. In some situations attitudes may be more important determinants of behavioural intentions than subjective norms, but in other situations more weight may be given to behaving in a normative way rather than in a way in accord with personal attitudes.

It is important to recognise that this model does not dismiss other factors such as situational, demographic or personality influences; it simply sees them as being mediated by the two major components. Perhaps certain personality types may be more likely to give weight to social normative pressures, or maybe some evaluative beliefs and personal values are a reflection of the socioeconomic, religious or ethnic context in which you were raised or live now. The theory argues that at present no other variables have been identified that can help consistently and reliably to provide a better explanation for people's rational behaviour than attitudes and subjective norms.

Behavioural intentions

Basically, the aim of the Theory of Reasoned Action is to relate beliefs to attitudes, attitudes to behavioural intentions and behavioural intentions to actual behaviour. Potentially this could be quite a nice way out of the difficulties posed by the oft-found poor relationship between attitudes and behaviour, which was discussed in Chapter 4. Before we go any further, it will be useful to stress at this point that the emphasis in this theory is on attitudes towards an act, towards some behaviour, *not* towards an object directly. So, for example, if I wanted to find out your attitude to this book I would look at your attitude to reading it rather than your attitude towards the book as an object. The book itself could be put to many uses and your attitude to it may differ accordingly.

Behavioural intentions precede behaviour but other factors may intervene before the intention is realised. I may leave home intending to purchase a given daily newspaper but notice the headline on a competing newspaper and decide to buy that one instead.

Or maybe I lose the money on the way to the shop. Or maybe I see someone collecting money for charity on the way and give the money to a good cause. Many things can happen to get in the way of a behavioural intention being realised. Getting around that problem was one of the major difficulties that had to be ironed out in the attitude–behaviour debate. This certainly seems a sensible solution. Behavioural intention usually has a far stronger and more reliable association with expressed attitudes than does overt behaviour.

In terms of the relationships between behaviour and behavioural intentions, two factors seem to be extremely important: the time gap between the expression of the behavioural intention and the actual behaviour, and the specificity with which the behavioural intention and actual behaviour are expressed.

Do it now!

In terms of the time gap between expressing a behavioural intention and acting on that intention, it probably seems a fairly reasonable assertion that the bigger the gap the less likely the intention is to be expressed. Obviously if I delay acting on my intention it leaves a gap in which a variety of other influences and distractions may cause me to change my attitudes, priorities and intentions. I may decide to buy one brand of chocolate but then see an advert and go for a different brand, or eat a meal and not feel like eating chocolate at all. Although these are anecdotal examples, you may recall my discussion of empirical research on the role of fear in persuasive communications (Chapter 5), which also confirmed that the sooner a behavioural intention is acted on, the more likely it is to be predictive of actual behaviour. People made afraid of the consequences of poor dental hygiene are more likely to go and see a dentist when they are encouraged to make an immediate appointment than when they simply express an intention to do so in the future.

Be specific!

An important aspect of the Theory of Reasoned Action is its emphasis that factors must be measured at the same level of specificity. A consumer's attitude towards a general product type, such as convenience foods, is not likely to be a good basis for predicting the purchase of a specific product on a specific day at a specific price. How many of us have heard people exclaim that they cannot be prejudiced because some of their friends belong to a minority group? The fallacy of arguing from the general to the particular is obvious. Because a large machine is heavy it does not mean that each of its components is! The more precisely an attitude is measured, the more likely it is to be related to a specific behavioural intention. In turn, the more precisely a behavioural intention is specified, the more likely it is to be predictive of actual behaviour.

To be useful, behavioural intentions and behaviour must be assessed at the same level of specificity. In a study of a weight loss programme, Ajzen and Fishbein (1980) illustrate the importance of specificity in the Theory of Reasoned Action. Obesity is a common problem and both diet and physical exercise are likely to be important in weight loss. Both should be given consideration. Of course diet and exercise are general categories and we have already noted that these can be difficult to work with. So specific acts were determined under each of these general headings, as well as a general measure of the intention to lose weight and general measures to engage in dieting and physical activity. As examples of the specific measures of behavioural intention, participants in the study rated items such as 'I intend to avoid snacking between meals and in the evenings for the next two months' and 'I intend to do exercises, such as jogging or callisthenics, on a regular basis for the next two months.' The overall result was that the intention to diet and the intention to engage in physical activity were both related to specific behavioural intentions which in turn were related to actual behaviours. In contrast, the general intentions to diet and engage in physical activity were substantially less closely related to actual behaviour. Of course, all this shows is the extent to which behavioural intentions are translated into actual behaviour. The study does go on to look at the extent to which these behaviours did actually bring about weight loss (dieting seemed to be quite successful and was a significant predictor; physical activity was not), although this is another question – whether the behaviours you intend to engage in will actually bring about the result you want!

Attitudes towards an act

The attitude towards an act may itself be seen as being composed of the sum of a series of evaluatively weighted beliefs. To make this a bit more concrete, the belief would be the perceived likelihood that the act is related to some object value or goal. So, for example, I may have a strong belief that taking an aspirin will relieve my headache. But this will also have a value to me. If I have a headache, then losing it probably has great value to me. So this evaluatively weighted belief may be an important determinant of my intended behaviour. I very probably would have the intention to take an aspirin if I had a headache. Of course other beliefs may be less strongly held. I may also believe that simply increasing my fluid intake would improve my headache, though the likelihood may be lower and so I am more likely to opt for the aspirin alternative. Of course an attitude may not consist of just one evaluatively weighted belief. Perhaps I also have reservations about taking medicinal drugs, and so those evaluatively weighted beliefs would also have to be added into the equation. Only when we have added together the range of positive and negative beliefs that we hold about an act can we have a clear picture of our overall attitude.

So, how would the above description of how we could measure an attitude towards an act work in practice? Typically a researcher may initially identify a set of beliefs about a given act, such as voting for political party X (insert the party of your own choice). Each of these beliefs is then rated for belief strength (how likely they are). So, for example, a statement about the political party may go something along the lines of 'voting for this party would lead to an increase in taxation', and the respondent may be required to rate it on a 7-point scale, say from -3 (highly unlikely) to $+3$ (very likely). They would be given a similar scale to assess the value they attach to the belief (how important taxation level is to them). Each rating of each belief would be multiplied by the evaluative rating to produce a score for that statement. Add all the statement scores together and you have the overall attitude score.

From these examples you can see that both the strength of a belief and its associated evaluation are determinants of an attitude. The implication is that we can potentially change someone's attitude through changing either or both of these components – by changing their beliefs about an act, or by changing how they evaluate these beliefs. My attitude towards taking a tablet to cure an illness would be very different if I was told it was 100 per cent certain it would have the promised effect, in comparison to if I were told it was only 10 per cent certain it would have an effect. Similarly, my attitude towards taking the tablet might differ if it was promising a total cure rather than just partial relief.

Salience of beliefs

As has already been mentioned, there is potentially an infinite number of beliefs that a person can hold about any act. It would be an impossibility to identify and measure them all. Fortunately the Theory of Reasoned Action does not require that we do this. All we are required to do is to take account of those beliefs that are salient for the individual at the time the attitude is measured. Smokers, for example, do differ from non-smokers in the beliefs that are important to them about smoking and in their evaluations of the positive and negative consequences of the act (van Harreveld *et al.*, 1999).

In practical terms, salience is usually defined as the first beliefs that an individual reports in answer to an open-ended (i.e. non-directive) question about an act. Note that the individual is not asked which beliefs are important or should be taken into account. All that is required is the reporting of the first beliefs and associations that come to mind when questioned. The fact that a belief is reported first is taken to indicate that it is salient for the individual. In effect, the order in which respondents report their beliefs tells us which beliefs are most significant for them at the time of questioning. Empirical evidence suggests that it is the first seven or so beliefs produced in this way that are most influential in forming attitudes. This could reflect natural limits of short-term memory.

Of course, shifts in the salience of beliefs may occur over time or due to situational factors, and these may underpin some of the apparent changes and inconsistencies we sometimes see in people's attitudes. This is a notion not dissimilar to that of agenda setting, which we have previously discussed (see Chapter 2). By making certain beliefs salient we may be influencing a person's attitude and potentially their behaviour (Iyengar and Kinder, 1987).

Putting it all together – an example

Just to show the mechanics of how we might assess an attitude, I will use the hypothetical example of going out for a curry with friends. Let's assume we question someone about this activity and find four salient beliefs, listed below. We could then ask the person to rate each belief for its likelihood (B) and importance or evaluation (E). We might find a set of results like those below. The respondent seems to believe that it is quite likely that the curry will be enjoyed, and this is a very important consideration. Even more likely, and equally important, is that the company will be enjoyed. It is also quite likely that this person will enjoy a drink with their meal and that the meal will be moderately priced, although these are only moderately important considerations.

Overall, on a scale that could run from -36 to $+36$, the score of $+23$ represents a moderately positive attitude. Try adjusting some of the beliefs and evaluations for yourself and see

Attitude towards going for a curry with friends

Belief	B	E	$B \times E$
Will enjoy the taste	2	3	6
Will enjoy the company	3	3	9
Will enjoy a drink with the meal	2	2	4
It will be moderately priced	2	2	4
		Total:	23

what it does to the overall attitude score. But even with a relatively positive attitude such as this, we still may not actually go out for the curry. Maybe we feel that it is expected that we will stay in that night to prepare for tomorrow's seminar ... That brings me neatly to the second factor influencing behavioural intentions, subjective norms.

Subjective norms

Just as the attitude component of the Theory of Reasoned Action can be broken down, so can the subjective norms component – although this has received considerably less research attention and does seem to be somewhat less clearly specified.

The first component of a person's subjective norms is their social normative beliefs. This is what they believe other relevant and significant people expect them to do – the perceived likelihood that these other people will approve of the action. The second component is their motivation to comply. We all know of some teenagers who know precisely what is expected of them but have very little motivation to comply. Indeed, sometimes the motivation is definitely *not* to comply!

It is widely accepted that there are difficulties with the subjective norms factor, particularly with the motivation to comply component, and most markedly with regard to measurement issues. Potentially each of the factors in the subjective norm equation could be measured on a scale similar to that described for measuring attitudinal beliefs and evaluations, although measuring the motivational component in this way may be particularly questionable and it is sometimes simply omitted.

Criticisms of the Theory of Reasoned Action

Before embarking on a review of some of the criticisms that have been made against the Theory of Reasoned Action, it is appropriate to note that there is also a considerable body of empirical evidence that has accumulated over several decades in support of the approach (Eagly and Chaiken, 1993).

As one might expect from a theory that has been around for quite some time, quite a number of criticisms have been raised against it. Some have been rejected out of hand as misinterpretations of the theory (e.g. Miniard and Cohen, 1981). Others are more substantial, and in this section I will review some of the more telling criticisms.

The limits of reasoned action

Several authors (e.g. Sarver, 1983; Sutton, 1987) have argued that an important limitation of the Theory of Reasoned Action is that it does not apply to other, more spontaneous behaviours such as emotional outbursts, well-learned, automatic skills, habitual behaviours (such as with drug addiction) and the like. Developing this idea, Fazio and Towles-Schwen (1999) argue that the relationship between attitudes and behaviour may take two forms. In the first, a specific behaviour may be chosen after an explicit analysis of costs and benefits and taking into account existing attitudes. Alternatively, behaviour may be more spontaneous, and attitudes may essentially be in the background and their influence may be largely unrecognised by the individual. Although it is worth highlighting the limits of the theory, Ajzen and Fishbein did, of course, only intend their approach to cover deliberate, rationally chosen behaviours. So the issue may be the extent to which we can actually distinguish between these thought-through and spontaneous forms of behaviour. Liska (1984) argues that to distinguish volitional behaviour (not requiring skills, abilities, opportunities and co-operation), which the Theory of Reasoned Action explains, from other forms of behaviour is neither simple nor tenable. He argues that behaviour falls on a continuum rather than into two neat categories of volitional and non-volitional. Similarly, resources, whether material or personal abilities and skills, are likely to be a crucial element and should be included. It is interesting to note how the Theory of Planned Behaviour, discussed later in this chapter, has gone some way towards recognising this criticism, with the incorporation of the factor of perceived behavioural control.

Blocks to behavioural intentions

It has been argued (Sarver, 1983) that the Theory of Reasoned Action gives insufficient consideration to factors that may block the expression of a behavioural intention. These may be a variety of unforeseen circumstances, actual blocks, or possibly more attractive alternatives that become available. It is perhaps true that the output end of the equation could be given more consideration, though this does not reduce the value of the theory construction that has already been completed.

Turning to a more empirical critique, a study by Shepherd and O'Keefe (1984) examined the extent to which the attitudinal and normative components of the Theory of Reasoned Action were genuinely two distinct entities in their influence on behavioural intentions. They found a substantial correlation between the two components, and this was often greater than the correlation either component had with behavioural intentions. Although it would not be wise to over-generalise these findings, it does none the less appear that the normative and attitudinal components of the model may not always be clearly separable.

The cost of keeping things simple

One of the more substantial critical reviews of the Theory of Reasoned Action comes from Liska (1984), who makes a number of important criticisms. First, he argues that narrowing the model down to two variables, attitudes and subjective norms, may cause problems. Because a whole host of other factors are seen as working through these two main components, these main variables may be made less stable. But if these other factors are separated out, then the model no longer has one of its main virtues – simplicity. Focusing on beliefs, Liska suggests that a more sophisticated, multi-method approach to their measurement may be more appropriate than relying on simple semantic differential-type scales. Beliefs may be too complex to be measured on a simple affective dimension. Liska suggests that more sophisticated measurement techniques may show that beliefs affect behavioural intentions and behaviour directly as well as through attitudes. Similarly, attitudes may also be the result of factors other than beliefs (e.g. the result of conditioning). Moving a little way along the equation, Liska also comments on the use of behavioural intentions as a mediator between attitudes and behaviour. He argues that studies are inconsistent about whether behavioural intentions or other components are better predictors. Often laboratory studies support behavioural intentions and field studies do not. Liska suggests that behavioural intentions do not totally mediate the effects of attitudes and can be unstable – that is, dependent on situational factors and less predictive the greater the time interval before measurement. Doesn't this bring back fond memories of the old attitude–behaviour debate! Finally, Liska criticises the Theory of Reasoned Action for showing little theoretical interest in the influence of behaviour on attitudes (as in cognitive-dissonance-type effects), although Ajzen and Fishbein do not dispute the existence of such reciprocal effects. Liska argues that these reciprocal effects are not something that can simply be ignored, and if they are not taken into account then the effect of behavioural intentions on behaviour will be a biased estimate.

Liska's criticisms of the Theory of Reasoned Action are substantial, especially his attack on the central position of the behavioural intentions component. A study by Davis (1985) attempted to test Liska's idea. Although Davis found empirical evidence that gave some support to Liska, he did not find that behavioural intention lost its position of central importance.

Some theorists have attempted to produce a two-component model as an alternative to the unidimensional Theory of Reasoned Action, giving separate emphasis to the cognitive and evaluative components of attitudes (e.g. Bagozzi and Burnkrant, 1985), though research supporting such a re-conceptualisation has been severely criticised on methodological and statistical grounds (Dillon and Kumar, 1985).

Further developments – the Theory of Planned Behaviour

Despite the many criticisms over the years, the Theory of Reasoned Action is still going strong. However, it does have a more recent, more complex, incarnation – the Theory of Planned Behaviour.

You may recall that in discussing Rogers's (1975, 1983) Protection Motivation Theory an important revision to the early version of the theory was the inclusion of a 'self-efficacy' factor: the extent to which the person believed that they were able to effectively execute the necessary coping response. The Theory of Planned Behaviour represents a similar amendment to the original Theory of Reasoned Action. The Theory of Planned Behaviour (Ajzen, 1985) emphasises the role of perceived behavioural control as an influence on behavioural intentions and actual behaviour. A person's confidence (or lack of it) in their ability to perform the required behaviour may be a crucial determinant of whether they choose to undertake the behaviour and are successful in its execution. The perceived behavioural control of a person who is uncertain of their ability to execute a behaviour may be influenced by their perception of their personal resources, such as their own abilities, their self-esteem and confidence, and the time and money that are required to be successful. For example, in sports we often hear of the gifted athlete who is constantly runner-up in competitions but never quite seems able to take the final hurdle and win outright. Perhaps at least part of the reason for this failure is that small doubt in their mind over their own behavioural control, over their ability to perform at the required level and triumph. Similar examples could be made in relation to people attempting to be successful on diets or perhaps in alcohol or drugs rehabilitation programmes. Studies comparing the Theory of Reasoned Action and the Theory of Planned Behaviour suggest that the extended Theory of Planned Behaviour may be a significantly better predictor of behavioural intentions and behaviour than is the Theory of Reasoned Action (Madden *et al.*, 1992).

The Elaboration Likelihood Model of persuasion

Although I have previously discussed the impact of various characteristics of messages on their recall and retention, it may be that in real life these have relatively little effect on attitudes and behaviour. We probably find most advertisements reasonably easy to comprehend and yet they do not necessarily persuade us. So what makes the difference? Some theorists have argued that a major consideration is the way in which a persuasive message is cognitively processed, and this may be determined by our involvement, knowledge and interest in the area of concern.

This approach to attitude change emphasises that the thoughts that arise in the persuasion situation are likely to be crucial determinants of any attitude change. If these thoughts are positive then they may promote attitude change in the direction advocated; if negative then they may actually have the opposite effect to that advocated. Note that this idea is closely related to the notion of psychological reactance, discussed in Chapter 5.

Measuring cognitive responses

There are many cognitive theories of persuasion, and also many ideas about what constitutes an appropriate measure of cognitive response. One widely accepted approach is the thought listing technique. In this approach, experimental subjects will typically be given a specified amount of time to list all the thoughts that occur to them before, during, or after exposure to the persuasive communication. Other subjects or judges, blind to the purpose of the experiment, then categorise the responses along one or more dimensions appropriate to the purpose of the study. For example, they may be categorised as favourable, unfavourable or neutral thoughts about the persuasive communication.

The thought listing technique has been used in a variety of guises in cognitive response research. It has been the main outcome measure, and it has been used as a check that experimental manipulations have been effective, and as a measure of the processes mediating persuasion.

Cognitive effort and ability

A major principle of the cognitive response approach is that an individual's motivation to process a message will affect their patterns of information processing. These effects will be reflected in the thought listing technique discussed above. Petty and Cacioppo (1986) argue that conditions such as a high level of involvement with an issue will motivate an individual to pay close attention to the content and quality of a persuasive message. In other words, under these conditions individuals would be expected to exert greater cognitive effort, and this should be reflected in the number of message-relevant thoughts that are elicited by the thought listing technique. To make this more concrete, let's assume that a persuasive message argues in favour of more unseen examinations for students. You may not pay that message too much attention unless you are a student – in which case you will probably scrutinise it very closely indeed.

By examining the factors that influence the amount of cognitive effort that individuals devote to processing persuasive messages, one can start to specify the conditions under which the quality of arguments in a message will be a significant factor in persuasion. And, of course, the contrary also applies: one can potentially identify those situations in which factors other than message quality (e.g. characteristics of the source) may be the main determinants of persuasion.

As an example of cognitive effort let us look at a study of the consequences of identifying multiple sources in persuasive communication. It is often found that when a number of arguments are presented by separate sources there is a higher level of persuasion than when all the arguments are presented by one source. A study by Harkins and Petty (1981) found that with multiple sources experimental subjects reported more message-relevant thoughts. Note that this may or may not be to the advantage of the communicator. With added attention to the arguments it is likely that there will be more negative thoughts and the arguments will be rejected if they are weak. So it seems that the extra cognitive effort aroused by multiple sources may underpin changes in persuasion resulting from the use of multiple sources. To confirm this, Harkins and Petty found that a distraction that prevented the extra cognitive processing eliminated the effect of multiple sources, even if participants can still remember and comprehend the arguments presented. This and other studies show that persuasion is more dependent on argument quality when contextual factors allow or encourage participants to increase the effort they devote to the cognitive processing of a persuasive communication.

Types of persuasion

In the Elaboration Likelihood Model (Petty and Cacioppo, 1981) there are two routes through which persuasion may occur, usually termed the central and peripheral routes. A similar model of persuasion has been proposed by Chaiken (1987), who characterises these two routes to persuasion as entailing systematic and heuristic processing.

The central route involves the active processing of the message itself. Attitude change brought about through this route is likely to be stronger and more persistent (Petty et al., 1995). This has been the focus of most research on the cognitive response approach to persuasion. As we have already seen, individuals are likely to use this route when they are motivated to think about an attitude issue, such as when it has personal relevance. As such conditions produce greater cognitive effort and elaboration, the quality of the arguments in the message is likely to be of crucial importance. Factors preventing or disrupting message relevant thinking (e.g. distractions) will reduce effects via the central route. This may be why some advertisements use humour, music and celebrities; in addition to their own persuasive impacts they may distract us from focusing too much on the message itself.

The peripheral route to persuasion is used when there is minimal cognitive elaboration of a message, and non-message factors are largely responsible for any attitude change that occurs. For example, source factors such as credibility or physical attractiveness may achieve their effects through the peripheral route. The peripheral route to persuasion mainly occurs when a recipient's motivation or ability to process the content of a message is low.

An experimental example of the routes to persuasion

A study by Petty, Cacioppo and Goldman (1981) examined the effects of personal involvement (relevance), argument quality and source expertise on undergraduate students' attitudes towards the introduction of comprehensive final examinations. Relevance was manipulated by stating that the examinations would be introduced at the university the following year (highly relevant to current students) or in ten years' time (considerably less relevant as it would affect none of the current student population). Argument quality was manipulated by having the participants listen to either eight strong arguments or eight weak arguments in favour of the proposal. Source expertise was manipulated by telling the participants that the tape they would hear was based on a report prepared either by a local high school class (low status) or by the prestigious Carnegie Commission on Higher Education.

As predicted, persuasion was only affected by high-quality arguments (the central route) when personal relevance was high. With low relevance, source expertise (the peripheral route) was the most significant determinant of persuasion. This provides strong support for Petty and Cacioppo's contention that involvement is an important determinant of the route or type of cognitive processing that an individual is likely to adopt when dealing with a persuasive message. It is worth noting the relevance of this finding for advertising. We have relatively little personal interest and involvement in most advertising, and so factors that are used in the peripheral route to processing (high-status sources, attractive characters, famous actors, humour, music, etc.) may be especially important, possibly a lot more so than any detailed information about the product concerned.

The Petty and Cacioppo versus Stiff debate

One of the most severe critiques of the Elaboration Likelihood Model of persuasion was put forward by James Stiff (1986). What followed was a very detailed debate which, while not fully favouring one view or the other, enabled a considerable clarification of the two theories. In the end, the differences appeared far less than when the debate started. It will be instructive to examine this debate in detail.

The opening shot

Stiff (1986) argued that Petty and Cacioppo's Elaboration Like-lihood Model is, in effect, a single channel, limited capacity model which assumes that individuals are forced to choose between central and peripheral routes for processing persuasive informa-tion. He noted that Petty and Cacioppo had demonstrated a relationship between issue involvement and central processing, but argued that they had not shown how low involvement produces peripheral processing.

Stiff proposed an alternative model based on Kahneman's (1973) elastic capacity view of information processing. From this perspective, people are multi-channel limited capacity processors. They can process on several channels in parallel, but only up to the limit of their cognitive capacity. From this perspective the effort exerted increases in accordance with task difficulty until it peaks and levels out. Thus at low levels processing can occur on more than one level or channel, but very difficult tasks involving primary processing may take up all the available capacity and leave none for secondary processing. This model can predict parallel and sequential forms of information processing under different circumstances and is generally consistent with research findings on arousal and attention.

Based on an extension of Kahneman's model, Stiff hypothe-sised a positive relationship between involvement and the impact of central cues, and a curvilinear relationship between involvement and the effect of peripheral cues. To test these hypotheses, Stiff conducted a meta-analytic review of nineteen previous studies in the area. Meta-analysis is simply a method of statistically combin-ing previous research so that, in effect, it is like having one giant study. The results of the meta-analysis appeared to broadly con-firm Stiff's hypotheses. With low involvement there was little processing of either peripheral or central cues. With medium levels of involvement both types of cue were utilised; and with high levels of involvement it was mainly central cues that were used. This seemed to provide support for Stiff's alternative to the Elaboration Likelihood Model of persuasion, although it would not be a debate if the issue were settled with just one contribution.

The counterblast

In a reply to Stiff's critique, Petty, Kasmer, Haugtvedt and Cacioppo (1987) argued that many of Stiff's criticisms were based on a misinterpretation of their model. First, Petty *et al.* argued that Stiff was assuming that all message factors are central processing cues and all other variables (e.g. source factors) are peripheral cues. Petty *et al.* argued that the Elaboration Likelihood Model does not distinguish between central and peripheral cues. Instead they argued that variables may serve in one of three possible roles depending on the persuasion situation. One of these roles is as persuasive arguments (i.e. information), but they may also serve as cues (e.g. that more information implies more validity for that information) and as a basis for determining information-processing strategies (e.g. the information may lead you to make inferences about credibility). In other words, the same variable in different situations may serve different roles; it may be a 'central cue' in one context and a 'peripheral cue' in another.

In their second rebuttal Petty *et al.* argued that, contrary to Stiff's assertion, the Elaboration Likelihood Model does not preclude multi-channel processing.

Finally, Petty *et al.* criticised Stiff's meta-analysis. They argued that the way he organises the data is biased – for example, because he ignores the possibility of messages having effects on both central and peripheral processing.

The riposte

To a large extent the two journal articles mentioned above set out the positions of the opposing sides, though there were two final broadsides before the debate was drawn to a conclusion. In their reply to Petty *et al.*, Stiff and Boster (1987) argued that Petty's assertion that the Elaboration Likelihood Model does not preclude multi-channel processing is inadequate because, in effect, it makes their model untestable. They argued that specific predictions are needed and that the diagram in Petty *et al.*'s paper still seems to direct processing to one channel or the other. The conditions under which joint processing will occur need to be spelled out. They concluded this criticism by stating that research on the Elaboration Likelihood Model 'fails to emphasise parallel processing' (p. 251).

Stiff and Boster then turned their attention to Petty *et al.*'s argument that cues can have central or peripheral impact. Again they argued that this makes the model untestable and that one needs to be able to specify in advance whether a cue is central or peripheral. Otherwise one could obtain almost any result and simply explain it by some retrospective interpretation of how the persuasive message was processed.

Finally, in their last rather technical point, Stiff and Boster questioned the accuracy and procedures used in Petty *et al.*'s re-analysis of their meta-analytic study.

By this point you will have gathered that the debate has moved from broad issues to a concern with technical detail. It is already apparent that no one will come out as victor, but we should, for completeness, review the final contribution to the debate by Petty and his colleagues.

The last word – maybe

Petty, Cacioppo, Kasmer and Haugtvedt (1987) begin their final defence of the Elaboration Likelihood Model by noting that the Stiff and Boster article 'ignores many of the conceptual points made in our initial critique and continues to provide inaccurate characterizations of our research and writing' (p. 257).

Concerning the issue of parallel versus sequential processing, Petty *et al.* argue that this is not an issue that concerns them. They argue that the Elaboration Likelihood Model is a model of persuasion, and as such examines the effect of source, message and other factors but is not concerned with whether these are processed sequentially or in parallel. The issue of parallel versus sequential processing may be relevant to understanding cognitive processing in general, but it is not seen as necessary to the particular aim of understanding persuasion.

Perhaps an important aspect of this final contribution to the debate concerns the use of the terms 'peripheral cue' and 'central cue' by Stiff. Petty *et al.* argue that this is a mischaracterisation of their model. They talk about central and peripheral *routes* rather than *cues*. This would seem sensible, as they assert that information may be processed through either route in different circumstances. To all intents and purposes they are saying that there is no such thing as a central or peripheral cue, just a cue that may proceed through either the central or peripheral route. Within these routes to processing information a variety of processes may operate. For example, attitude change from the peripheral route may include classical conditioning, the use of simple decision rules and cognitive heuristics (short cuts that reduce the amount of cognitive processing of information that is required).

In response to the criticism that the multiple roles of source, message, and other factors render the model untestable, Petty *et al.* argue that they have made this situation explicit. The multiple roles may be complex but they can be accommodated in research. They note that they have published research showing source credibility serving argument, cue and directive roles in different situations.

In their final point, Petty *et al.* respond to Stiff's critique of their re-analysis of his meta-analysis. They point to the initial small sample on which the original meta-analysis was based and go into very fine detail in their methodological critique of Stiff's analyses. Petty *et al.* conclude by reiterating their assertion that it would be unwise to draw any conclusions based on a very small meta-analysis.

Conclusion

Would that the debate had concluded – it seemed largely to fizzle out! Stiff's critique has helped clarify aspects of the Elaboration Likelihood Model, and the model is still going strong. However, a number of more recent critiques have been made. Kruglanski and Thompson (1999) have recently proposed a single-route re-conceptualisation of dual-route models, which has attracted a great deal of attention and aroused considerable controversy. A substantial amount of research will need to be conducted before it becomes clear if this is tenable and represents a significant advance on existing models. There are undoubtedly still a great many theoretical and empirical issues to be clarified and resolved in our understanding of the cognitive bases of persuasion.

Summary

This chapter focused on two of the most influential models of persuasion, one having roots in behavioural psychology and one very firmly grounded in modern information-processing theory. Ajzen and Fishbein's Theory of Reasoned Action is a well-established approach of proven utility. It has made an important contribution to getting attitude research out of the attitude–behaviour impasse. Although a number of criticisms have been made of the theory, it has proved to be very robust. A recent extension to the theory – the Theory of Planned Behaviour – has helped to increase the accuracy and predictive power of the approach. The second model discussed was the Elaboration Likelihood Model of Petty and Cacioppo. This model has been particularly useful in helping to clarify the different cognitive routes that may be taken when people process persuasive messages. This has enabled a new, more sophisticated conceptualisation of much of the traditional literature on source, message and audience effects on the attitude-change process.

Further reading

Petty, R. E. and Cacioppo, J. T. (1996) *Attitudes and persuasion: classic and contemporary approaches.* Boulder, CO: Westview Press. An extremely thorough and comprehensive review of attitude theories – probably much more than you'll need!

Petty, R. E. and Cacioppo, J. T. (1986) *Communication and persuasion: central and peripheral routes to attitude change.* New York: Springer-Verlag. A detailed account of the Elaboration Likelihood Model.

Ajzen, I. and Fishbein, M. (1980) *Understanding attitudes and predicting social behavior.* Englewood Cliffs, NJ: Prentice-Hall. A good summary of the Theory of Reasoned Action, a review of applications, and useful appendices giving step-by-step guidance for the construction of an attitude questionnaire and a sample questionnaire.

Glossary

affect Feelings and moods. The emotional component of an attitude.

argument A statement in a persuasive message that proposes a given stance or position on an issue.

arousal A physiological or psychological state of readiness for action.

attitude A person's relatively enduring positive or negative evaluation of some aspect of their world (object, action or person) that is of significance to them.

attitude accessibility The extent to which attitudes are automatically and easily retrieved from memory.

attitude–behaviour debate The ongoing controversy about the extent to which attitudes predict actual behaviour, and hence behaviour may be an integral component of attitudes.

attitude scale A set of statements with which respondents are asked to agree or disagree. Scales are designed to be relatively quick and easy to administer, often to groups. It is crucial that they are reliable and valid (see below for definitions of these terms).

133

attribution   The mechanism through which we infer the traits and intentions of others.

audience   The recipients of a persuasive communication.

behavioural intention   The intention to perform an act because of a specific attitude that is held. Seen as mediating the relationship between attitudes and actual behaviour.

behavioural psychology   An approach that focuses on observable behaviour and the mechanisms of learning.

belief   The perception of a relationship between two aspects of an individual's world.

bogus pipeline approach   A technique for assessing attitudes which misleads the respondent into believing that the researcher has an insight into their attitudes through a device similar to a lie-detector.

central route   A concept from the Elaboration Likelihood Model of persuasion. This route to persuasion emphasises the careful consideration and analysis of the quality and implications of persuasive arguments. It is most likely where the topic is of personal significance for the individual (cf. peripheral route).

channel of communication   The modality in which a message is presented (e.g. written, audio, face-to-face).

classical (Pavlovian) conditioning   A behavioural approach which emphasises the learning of associations between neutral stimuli and a stimulus with existing significance for the individual, with the consequence that the former acquire significance in their own right.

cognition   The component of attitudes emphasising an individual's thoughts, knowledge and understanding.

cognitive consistency theories   A major group of theories that emphasise that we actively seek consistency (or consonance) within and between our attitudes (cf. cognitive dissonance).

cognitive dissonance   The uncomfortable state where an individual perceives a discrepancy or inconsistency between two cognitions or attitudes. This tension is seen as motivating efforts to reduce the dissonance by a variety of possible mechanisms.

cognitive response models   A family of attitude theories that stress that the way we respond to persuasive messages is determined by the salient thoughts they evoke.

commitment   The extent to which we feel the need to maintain and defend a decision or our stance on an issue.

communication   The transmission of information.

consensual validation   The social affirmation of an individual's attitudes, beliefs or abilities (see also social comparison). Most common where objective means of validation are not possible.

demand effect   People behaving in response to cues which indicate what is expected of them in a given situation – for example, attempting to perform in an experiment in a way that they believe is expected.

discourse analysis   The analysis of the role of language in social interaction, and in constructing the way we see ourselves and our world.

discrimination   Prejudicial behaviour towards another person on the basis of some identifiable characteristic or group membership.

dizygotic twin   Non-identical twins, originating from two separate fertilised eggs (cf. monozygotic).

downward comparison   Social comparison (see below) with someone who is inferior on some ability or characteristic. May be used to enhance self-esteem.

ego defence function   Attitudes serving to protect and enhance the individual's self-esteem.

Elaboration Likelihood Model   A cognitive response model of persuasion proposed by Petty and Cacioppo (1981). It argues that persuasion may take two routes: central or peripheral (see above and below).

elastic capacity model   A model of persuasion which argues that the central and peripheral processing (see above and below) of a persuasive message may occur in parallel. The weight accorded each of the two types of processing is seen as depending on the individual's involvement with the issue concerned.

functional approach   A theoretical approach to understanding attitudes that emphasises the functions they serve for the individual rather than their structure.

information-processing models   Cognitive approaches that emphasise how information is manipulated by the individual.

instrumental (operant) conditioning   A behavioural theory that emphasises that behaviour is under the control of its consequences. Positive (rewarding) consequences are seen as increasing the strength and probability of a response.

instrumental (also adjustive or utilitarian) function   Attitudes serving this function help the individual to maximise their rewards.

item   Statement or question on an attitude scale or questionnaire.

item analysis   The process by which attitude scale and questionnaire items are evaluated and weak items are removed or discounted.

knowledge function   Attitudes serving this function make our world more understandable, they give meaning to people, objects and events and make our world more predictable.

latitude of acceptance/rejection   Refers to the fact that the distance between our existing attitude and the position advocated by a persuasive message will affect the likelihood of attitude change occurring. The difference between our existing attitude and an advocated position that is acceptable and may result in attitude change will be greater for attitudes that are relatively unimportant to us and smaller for attitudes that have personal significance or are more extreme.

Likert scale   A type of attitude scale where respondents are presented with a series of items which are rated for agreement or disagreement. A respondent's attitude score is the sum of their ratings.

mass media   Modes of communication directed at large-scale audiences (e.g. television, radio, newspapers).

mere exposure effect   Refers to the fact that repeated exposure to a person or object may affect our attitude towards it – usually positively.

message   The informational content of a communication.

message learning approach   An approach to explaining persuasion that emphasises the factors that influence the attention, comprehension and acceptance of a message.

model   The person performing a behaviour that is imitated.

modelling (observational/vicarious learning)   Learning a behaviour through observing and imitating another person.

monozygotic twin   Identical twin; originating from a single fertilised egg (cf. dizygotic).

peripheral route   A concept from the Elaboration Likelihood Model of persuasion. This route to persuasion is based on the use of simple, superficial cues (e.g. characteristics of the person advocating attitude change). It is a short-cut route to attitude change which requires relatively little involvement or cognitive processing on the part of the recipient (cf. central route). It is most likely to be used in dealing with issues that are relatively unimportant to the individual.

persuasion   The process by which a person is influenced to change their attitudes and opinions.

prejudice   An attitude, usually negative, towards a person because of their personal characteristics or group membership (e.g. on the basis of race or gender).

primacy An effect whereby information encountered first is better remembered or more influential than information encountered subsequently (cf. recency).

projective techniques Indirect methods of attitude and personality assessment that present respondents with ambiguous stimuli on which they are encouraged to impose their own meanings and interpretations.

Protection Motivation Theory An SEU (see below) model of attitude change that attempts to explain respondents' reactions to fear-based health messages.

psychological reactance The tendency for people to attempt to restore their perceived freedom of choice and action when they believe it to be threatened.

recency An effect whereby information encountered recently is better remembered or more influential than information encountered earlier (cf. primacy).

related attributes hypothesis The idea, in social comparison theory, that we select others who are similar to ourselves, in terms of attributes we see as significant and relevant (e.g. age or sex), as the basis for evaluating our other attitudes, characteristics and abilities.

reliability Relates to the consistency of an attitude scale or item; the likelihood of obtaining the same result on a second occasion.

reward Any event following a response that increases the subsequent probability or strength of that response.

salience In the Theory of Reasoned Action, this refers to the first thoughts and beliefs that come to mind after a persuasive communication.

scalogram analysis A type of attitude scale in which the items are rank ordered. Thus respondents should agree with all items up to a specific point and then no others. Consequently, knowing the last item a person agreed with tells you which other items were agreed with or disagreed with.

self-concept An individual's set of beliefs about him or herself.

self-esteem The evaluative aspect of the self-concept. How we believe we stand relative to our aspirations and how we would ideally like to be.

Self-Perception Theory An alternative explanation of cognitive dissonance phenomena which argues that an individual's reported attitudes are derived from their observation of their own behaviour.

SEU See Subjected Expected Utility.

social comparison The mechanism whereby we compare our own attitudes and abilities with those of others in order to achieve consensual validation (see above).

social distance scale An attempt to measure social attitudes by presenting respondents with a series of alternatives of varying degrees of positivity. They are required to indicate which they agree with, or the extent of their agreement. This allows a simple and intuitive ordering of respondents with regard to their attitude to the object of concern.

sociometry A technique for measuring social choice and popularity. At its simplest it simply consists of asking an individual to provide a list of people satisfying certain criteria (e.g. friend).

source The person, group or institution seen as the originator of a communication.

stimulus Any event evoking a response from an organism.

Subjective Expected Utility (SEU) A broad theoretical approach that sees individuals as striving to maximise their rewards and minimise the aversive outcomes resulting from their behaviour.

subjective norm In the Theory of Reasoned Action, one of the components determining behavioural intentions. Comprised of the expectations that we believe others hold and our motivation to comply with these.

subliminal conditioning The classical conditioning of attitudes below the level of awareness.

subliminal perception The perception of a stimulus below the level of awareness.

theory An explanation of the relationship between a set of observed events.

Theory of Planned Action A successor to the Theory of Reasoned Action which acknowledges the role of a person's confidence in their ability to perform an act as a determinant of behavioural intentions and success.

Theory of Reasoned Action A theory attempting to explain the relationship between attitudes and behaviour. Attitudes are seen as evaluatively weighted beliefs. These, together with subjective norms, affect behavioural intentions. Behavioural intentions are seen as the major direct determinant of actual behaviour.

Thurstone scale A type of attitude scale where each item has a specific value. The respondent's attitude score is the median value of all those items with which agreement is expressed.

triadic (also known as classical or ABC) model of attitudes   A model presenting attitudes as having three closely connected components: affect, behaviour, and cognition.

two-factor theory of emotion   The idea that the experience of emotion has a physiological basis but that the labelling of the experience is, at least in part, a function of cognitive appraisal and may reflect social and situational influences.

two-step flow theory   An approach to explaining the persuasive effects of the mass media. It argues that mass media effects on most individuals are indirect, mediated by active, well-informed opinion leaders within groups.

upward comparison   Social comparison (see above) with others who are superior on some ability or characteristic (e.g. sporting ability), or who are members of an admired group. May be motivated by a desire for self-improvement.

validity   The extent to which an item or scale measures what it purports to measure.

value-expressive function   Attitudes serve this function if they support and are an integral part of the individual's self-concept. Having these values and attitudes affirmed is a source of satisfaction to the individual.

volition   The individual's perceived freedom of choice and action.

References

Aguinis, H. and Handelsman, M. M. (1997) Ethical
issues in the use of the bogus pipeline. *Journal
of Applied Social Psychology*, 27, 574–581.

Aguinis, H., Pierce, C. A. and Quigley, B. M. (1993)
Conditions under which a bogus pipeline procedure enhances the validity of self-reported
cigarette smoking: a meta-analytic review.
Journal of Applied Social Psychology, 23,
352–373.

Ajzen, I. (1985) From intentions to actions: a theory
of planned behavior. In: J. Kuhland and
J. Beckman (eds), *Action-control: from cognitions to behaviour.* Heidelberg, Germany:
Springer.

Ajzen, I. and Fishbein, M. (1980) *Understanding
attitudes and predicting social behaviour.*
London: Prentice-Hall.

Allport, G. (1954) The historical background of
modern social psychology. In: G. Lindzey (ed.),
*Handbook of social psychology, vol. 1: Theory
and method.* Reading, MA: Addison-Wesley.

REFERENCES

Anastasi, A. and Urbina, S. (1997) *Psychological testing* (7th edn). Englewood Cliffs, NJ: Prentice-Hall.

Aronson, E. (1968) Dissonance theory: progress and problems. In: R. P. Abelson, E. Aronson, W. J. McGuire, T. M. Newcomb, M. J. Rosenberg and P. H. Tannenbaum (eds), *Theories of cognitive consistency: a source-book*. Chicago: Rand-McNally.

Augoustinos, M. (1991) Consensual representations of social structure in different age groups. *British Journal of Social Psychology, 30*, 193–205.

Bagozzi, R. P. and Burnkrant, R. E. (1985) Attitude organisation and the attitude–behavior relation. A reply to Dillon and Kumar. *Journal of Personality and Social Psychology, 49*, 47–57.

Bales, R. F. and Cohen, S. P. (1979) *SYMLOG: a system for the multiple level observation of groups*. Chicago: University of Chicago Press.

Bandura, A. (1971) Analysis of modeling processes. In: A. Bandura (ed.), *Psychological modeling: conflicting theories*. Chicago: Aldine-Atherton.

Bem, D. (1967) Self-perception: an alternative interpretation of cognitive dissonance phenomena. *Psychological Review, 74*, 183–200.

Bem, D. (1968) Attitudes as self-descriptions: another look at the attitude behavior link. In: A. G. Greenwald, T. C. Brock and T. M. Ostrom (eds), *Psychological foundations of attitudes*. New York: Academic Press.

Bogardus, E. S. (1925) Measuring Social Distance. *Journal of Applied Sociology, 9*, 299–308.

Bornstein, F. R. (1989) Exposure and affect: overview and meta-analysis of research 1968–1987. *Psychological Bulletin, 106*, 265–289.

Boster, F. J. and Mongeau, P. (1984) Fear-arousing persuasive messages. In: R. M. Bostrom (ed.), *Communication yearbook, vol. 8*. Beverly Hills, CA: Sage.

Bradac, J. J., Hemphill, M. R. and Tardy, C. H. (1981) Language style on trial. Effects of powerful and powerless speech on judgements of victims and villains. *Western Journal of Speech Communication, 45*, 327–341.

Breckler, S. J. (1984) Empirical validation of affect, behavior and cognition as distinct components of attitude. *Journal of Personality and Social Psychology, 47*, 1191–1205.

Brehm, S. S. and Brehm, J. W. (1981) *Psychological reactance: a theory of freedom and control*. New York: Academic Press.

Brehm, J. W. and Cohen, A. R. (1962) *Explorations in cognitive dissonance*. New York: Wiley.

Brown, R., Vivian, J. and Hewstone, M. (1999) Changing attitudes through intergroup contact: the effects of group membership salience. *European Journal of Social Psychology*, 29, 741–764.

Brown, S. (1999) Public attitudes toward the treatment of sex offenders. *Legal and Criminological Psychology*, 4, 239–252.

Byrne, D. (1971) *The attraction paradigm.* New York: Academic Press.

Calder, B. J., Insko, C. A. and Yandell, B. (1974) The relation of cognitive and memorial processes to persuasion in a simulated jury trial. *Journal of Applied Social Psychology*, 4, 62–93.

Campbell, A., Converse, P. E., Miller, W. E. and Stokes, D. E. (1960) *The American voter.* New York: Wiley.

Carli, L. L. (1990) Gender, language and influence. *Journal of Personality and Social Psychology*, 59, 941–951.

Chaiken, S. (1979) Communicator physical attractiveness and persuasion. *Journal of Personality and Social Psychology*, 37, 1387–1397.

Chaiken, S. (1987) The heuristic model of persuasion. In: M. P. Zanna, J. M. Olson and C. P. Herman (eds), *Social influence: the Ontario Symposium, vol. 5.* Hillsdale, NJ: Erlbaum.

Chaiken, S. and Eagly, A. H. (1976) Communication modality as a determinant of message persuasiveness and message comprehensibility. *Journal of Personality and Social Psychology*, 34, 605–614.

Chaiken, S. and Stangor, C. (1987) Attitudes and attitude change. *Annual Review of Psychology*, 38, 575–630.

Cheung, S. K. (1996) Cognitive-behaviour therapy for marital conflict: refining the concept of attribution. *Journal of Family Therapy*, 18, 183–203.

Cialdini, R. B. (1993) *Influence: science and practice* (3rd edn). New York: HarperCollins.

Cialdini, R. B. and Petty, R. E. (1981) Anticipatory opinion effects. In: R. E. Petty, T. M. Ostrom and T. C. Brock (eds), *Cognitive responses in persuasion.* Hillsdale, NJ: Erlbaum.

Cooper, J., Zanna, M. P. and Taves, P. A. (1978) Arousal as a necessary condition for attitude change following induced compliance. *Journal of Personality and Social Psychology*, 36, 1101–1106.

Crano, W. D. (1997) Vested interest, symbolic politics, and attitude-behaviour consistency. *Journal of Personality and Social Psychology*, 72, 485–491.

Croyle, D. T. and Cooper, J. (1983) Dissonance arousal: physiological evidence. *Journal of Personality and Social Psychology*, 45, 782–791.

Davis, R. A. (1985) Social structure, belief, attitude, intention and behavior: a partial test of Liska's revisions. *Social Psychology Quarterly*, *48*, 89–93.

DeFleur, M. L. and Westie, F. R. (1963) Attitude as a scientific concept. *Social Forces*, *42*, 17–31.

Dillon, W. R. and Kumar, A. (1985) Attitude organisation and the attitude–behavior relation: a critique of Bagozzi and Burnkrant's reanalysis of Fishbein and Ajzen. *Journal of Personality and Social Psychology*, *49*, 33–46.

Donofrio, B. M., Eaves, L. J., Murrelle, L., Maes, H. H. and Spilka, B. (1999) Understanding biological and social influences on religious affiliation, attitudes, and behaviors: a behavior genetic perspective. *Journal of Personality*, *67*, 953–984.

Eagly, A. H. (1974) Comprehensibility of persuasive arguments as a determinant of opinion change. *Journal of Personality and Social Psychology*, *29*, 758–773.

Eagly, A. H. (1978) Sex differences in influenceability. *Psychological Bulletin*, *85*, 86–116.

Eagly, A. H. and Chaiken, S. (1975) An attribution analysis of the effect of communicator characteristics on opinion change: the case of communicator attractiveness. *Journal of Personality and Social Psychology*, *32*, 136–144.

Eagly, A. H. and Chaiken, S. (1993) *The psychology of attitudes*. Fort Worth, TX: Harcourt Brace Jovanovich.

Eagly, A. H. and Warren, R. (1976) Intelligence, comprehension, and opinion change. *Journal of Personality*, *44*, 226–242.

Edwards, A. L. (1957) *Techniques of attitude scale construction*. New York: Appleton-Century-Crofts.

Edwards, A. L. and Kenny, K. C. (1946) A comparison of the Thurstone and Likert techniques of attitude scale construction. *Journal of Applied Psychology*, *30*, 72–83.

Elliot, A. J. and Devine, P. G. (1994) On the motivational nature of cognitive dissonance: dissonance as physiological discomfort. *Journal of Personality and Social Psychology*, *67*, 382–394.

Erwin, P. (1991) Attitudes. In: J. Radford and E. Govier (eds), *A textbook of psychology* (2nd edn). London: Routledge.

Erwin, P. G. and Hough, K. (1997) Children's attitudes toward violence on television. *Journal of Psychology*, *131*, 411–415.

Fabrigar, L. R. and Petty, R. E. (1999) The role of the affective and cognitive bases of attitudes in susceptibility to affectively and cognitively based persuasion. *Personality and Social Psychology Bulletin, 25,* 363–381.

Fabrigar, L. R., Priester, J. R., Petty, R. E. and Wegener, D. T. (1998) The impact of attitude accessibility on elaboration of persuasive messages. *Personality and Social Psychology Bulletin, 24,* 339–352.

Fazio, R. H. (1989) On the power and functionality of attitudes: the role of attitude accessibility. In: A. R. Pratkanis, S. J. Breckler and A. G. Greenwald (eds), *Attitude structure and function.* Hillsdale, NJ: Erlbaum.

Fazio, R. H. and Towles-Schwen, T. (1999) The mode model of attitude-behavior processes. In: S. Chaiken and Y. Trope (eds), *Dual process theories in social psychology.* New York: Guilford Press.

Fazio, R. H. and Zanna, M. P. (1981) Direct experience and attitude behaviour consistency. In: L. Berkowitz (ed.), *Advances in experimental social psychology, vol. 14.* New York: Academic Press.

Fazio, R. H., Ledbetter, J. E. and Towles-Schwen, T. (2000) On the costs of accessible attitudes: detecting that the attitude object has changed. *Journal of Personality and Social Psychology, 78,* 197–210.

Festinger, L. (1954) A theory of social comparison processes. *Human Relations, 7,* 117–140.

Festinger, L. (1957) A theory of cognitive dissonance. Stanford, CA: Stanford University Press.

Festinger, L. and Carlsmith, J. M. (1959) Cognitive consequences of forced compliance. *Journal of Abnormal and Social Psychology, 58,* 203–210.

Fishbein, M. and Ajzen, I. (1975) *Belief, attitude, intention, and behavior: an introduction to theory and research.* Reading, MA: Addison-Wesley.

Freedman, J. L., Cunningham, J. A. and Krismer, K. (1992) Inferred values and the reverse-incentive effect in induced compliance. *Journal of Personality and Social Psychology, 62,* 357–368.

Furnham, A. and Mak, T. (1999) Sex-role stereotyping in television commercials: a review and comparison of fourteen studies done on five continents over 25 years. *Sex Roles, 41,* 413–437.

Gauvin, L., Rejeski, W. J. and Norris, J. L. (1996) A naturalistic study of the impact of acute physical activity on feeling states and affect in women. *Health Psychology, 15,* 391–397.

Goethals G. R. and Darley, J. (1977) Social comparison theory: an attributional approach. In: J. M. Suls and R. M. Miller (eds),

145

Social comparison process: theoretical and empirical perspectives. Washington, DC: Hemisphere.

Greenwald, A. G., Pratkanis, A. R., Leippe, M. R. and Baumgardner, M. H. (1986) Under what conditions does theory obstruct research progress? *Psychological Review, 93,* 216–229.

Guttman, L. (1950) The basis for scalogram analysis. In: S. A. Stouffer (ed.), *Measurement and prediction.* Princeton, NJ: Princeton University Press.

Hadjimarcou, J. and Hu, M. Y. (1999). Global product stereotypes and heuristic processing: the impact of ambient task complexity. *Psychology and Marketing, 16,* 583–612.

Hall, C. C. I. and Crum, M. J. (1994) Women and 'body-isms' in television beer commercials. *Sex Roles, 31,* 329–337.

Hanson, D. J. (1980) Relationship between methods and findings in attitude-behaviour research. *Psychology, 17,* 11–13.

Harkins, S. G. and Petty, R. E. (1981) The multiple source effect in persuasion: the effects of distraction. *Personality and Social Psychology Bulletin, 7,* 627–635.

Hatfield, E. and Rapson, R. L. (1996) *Love and sex.* Boston, MA: Allyn & Bacon.

Hobden, K. L. and Olson, J. M. (1994) From jest to antipathy: disparagement humour as a source of dissonance motivated attitude change. *Basic and Applied Social Psychology, 15,* 239–249.

Hovland, C. I. and Weiss, W. (1951) The influence of source credibility on communication effectiveness. *Public Opinion Quarterly, 15,* 635–650.

Hovland, C., Lumsdaine, A. and Sheffield, F. (1949) *Experiments in mass communication.* Princeton, NJ: Princeton University Press.

Iyengar, S. and Kinder, D. R. (1987) *News that matters: agenda setting and priming in a television age.* Chicago: University of Chicago Press.

Jones, E. E. and Sigall, H. (1971) The bogus pipeline: a new paradigm for measuring affect and attitude. *Psychological Bulletin, 76,* 349–364.

Kahneman, D. (1973) *Attention and effort.* Englewood Cliffs, NJ: Prentice Hall.

Katz, D. (1960) The functional approach to the study of attitudes. *Public Opinion Quarterly, 24,* 163–204.

Katz, E. and Lazarsfeld, P. F. (1955) *Personal influence.* Glencoe, IL: Free Press.

Keefe, F. J. (2000) Self-Report of Pain: Issues and Opportunities. In: A. A. Stone and J. S. Turkkan (eds), *The science of self-report: implications for research and practice.* Mahwah, NJ: Erlbaum.

Krishnan, H. S. and Smith, R. E. (1998) The relative endurance of attitudes, confidence and attitude-behavior consistency. *Journal of Consumer Psychology*, 7, 273–298.

Krosnick, J. A., Betz, A. L., Jussim, L. J. and Lynn, A. R. (1992) Subliminal conditioning of attitudes. *Personality and Social Psychology Bulletin*, 18, 152–162.

Kruglanski, A. and Thompson, E. P. (1999) Persuasion by a single route: the Unimodel. *Psychological Inquiry*, 10, 83–109.

La Piere, R. T. (1934) Attitudes vs. actions. *Social Forces*, 13, 230–237.

Larson, C. V. (1992) *Persuasion: reception and responsibility* (6th edn). Belmont, CA: Wadsworth.

Lavine, H., Sweeney, D. and Wagner, S. H. (1999) Depicting women as sex objects in television advertising: effects on body dissatisfaction. *Personality and Social Psychology Bulletin*, 25, 1049–1058.

Leippe, M. R. and Eisenstadt, D. (1994) Generalization of dissonance reduction – decreasing prejudice through induced compliance. *Journal of Personality and Social Psychology*, 67, 395–413.

Leventhal, H. (1970) Findings and theory in the study of fear communications. In: L. Berkowitz (ed.), *Advances in experimental social psychology, vol. 5*. New York: Academic Press.

Likert, R. (1932) A technique for the measurement of attitudes. *Archives of Psychology*, No. 140.

Liska, A. E. (1984) A critical examination of the causal structure of the Fishbein/Ajzen attitude-behavior model. *Social Psychology Quarterly*, 47, 61–74.

Livneh, H. and Antonak, R. F. (1994) Indirect methods to measure attitudes toward persons with disabilities. *Rehabilitation Education*, 8, 103–137.

Lull, J. (1980) The social uses of television. *Human Communication Research*, 6, 197–209.

Lumsdaine, A. A. and Janis, I. L. (1953) Resistance to counter-propaganda produced by one-sided and two-sided propaganda presentations. *Public Opinion Quarterly*, 17, 311–318.

Lydon, J. E. and Zanna, M. P. (1990) Commitment in the face of adversity: a value-affirmation approach. *Journal of Personality and Social Psychology*, 58, 1040–1047.

McGuire, W. J. (1968) Personality and attitude change: an information processing theory. In: A. G. Greenwald, T. C. Brock and T. M. Ostrom (eds), *Psychological foundations of attitudes*. New York: Academic Press.

MacKenzie, S. B., Lutz, R. J. and Belch, G. E. (1986) The role of attitude towards the ad as a mediator of advertising effectiveness – a test of competing explanations. *Journal of Marketing Research, 23*, 2, 130–143.

McLuhan, M. (1964) *Understanding the media: the extensions of man.* New York: Signet Books.

Madden, T. J., Ellen, P. S. and Ajzen, I. (1992) A comparison of the Theory of Planned Behavior and the Theory of Reasoned Action. *Personality and Social Psychology Bulletin, 18*, 3–9.

Maio, G. R. and Olson, J. M. (2000) *Why we Evaluate: Functions of Attitudes.* Mahwah, NJ: Erlbaum.

Maio, G. R., Esses, V. M. and Bell, D. W. (1994) The formation of attitudes toward new immigrant groups. *Journal of Applied Social Psychology, 24*, 1762–1766.

Manstead, A. S. R. and McCulloch, C. (1981) Sex role stereotyping in British television advertisements. *British Journal of Social Psychology, 20*, 171–180.

Miller, C. T. (1984) Self-schemas, gender and social comparison: a clarification of the related attributes hypothesis. *Journal of Personality and Social Psychology, 46*, 1222–1229.

Miller, N. and Campbell, D. T. (1959) Recency and primacy in persuasion as a function of the timing of speeches and measurements. *Journal of Abnormal and Social Psychology, 59*, 1–9.

Mills, J. and Harvey, J. (1972) Opinion change as a function of when information about the communicator is received and whether he is attractive or expert. *Journal of Personality and Social Psychology, 21*, 52–55.

Miniard, P. and Cohen, J. B. (1981) An examination of the Fishbein-Ajzen behavioral intentions model's concepts and measures. *Journal of Experimental Social Psychology, 17*, 309–339.

Mita, T. H., Dermer, M. and Knight, J. (1977) Reversed facial images and the mere exposure hypothesis. *Journal of Personality and Social Psychology, 35*, 597–601.

Moreland, R. L. and Beach, S. R. (1992) Exposure effects in the classroom: the development of affinity among students. *Journal of Experimental Social Psychology, 28*, 255–276.

Moreno, J. L. (1953) *Who shall survive?* New York: Beacon House.

Mulheim, L. S., Allison, D. B., Heshka, S. and Heymsfield, S. B. (1998) Do unsuccessful dieters intentionally underreport food intake? *International Journal of Eating Disorders, 24*, 259–266.

Nezlek, J. B. (1999) Body image and day-to-day social interaction. *Journal of Personality*, 67, 793–817.

Oppenheim, A. N. (1992) *Questionnaire design, interviewing and attitude measurement*. London: Heinemann.

Patzer, G. L. (1985) *The physical attractiveness phenomenon*. New York: Plenum.

Perse, E. M. (1990) Involvement with local television news: cognitive and emotional dimensions. *Human Communication Research*, 16, 556–581.

Perse, E. M. and Rubin, A. M. (1990) Chronic loneliness and television use. *Journal of Broadcasting and Electronic Media*, 34, 37–53.

Petty, R. E. and Cacioppo, J. T. (1977) Forewarning, cognitive responding and resistance to persuasion. *Journal of Personality and Social Psychology*, 35, 645–655.

Petty, R. E. and Cacioppo, J. T. (1981) *Attitudes and persuasion: classic and contemporary approaches*. Dubuque, IA: WCB.

Petty, R. E. and Cacioppo, J. T. (1986) The Elaboration Likelihood Model of Persuasion. In: L. Berkowitz (ed.), *Advances in experimental social psychology, vol. 9*. New York: Academic Press.

Petty, R. E. and Krosnick, J. A. (1995) *Attitude Strength: Antecedents and Consequences*. Mahwah, NJ: Erlbaum.

Petty, R. E. and Wegener, D. T. (1998) Matching versus mismatching attitude functions: implications for scrutiny of persuasive messages. *Personality and Social Psychology Bulletin*, 24, 227–240.

Petty, R. E. and Wegener, D. T. (1999) The Elaboration Likelihood Model: current status and controversies. In: S. Chaiken and Y. Trope (eds), *Dual process theories in social psychology*. New York: Guilford Press.

Petty, R. E., Cacioppo, J. T. and Goldman, R. (1981) Personal involvement as a determinant of argument based persuasion. *Journal of Personality and Social Psychology*, 41, 847–855.

Petty, R. E., Cacioppo, J. T., Kasmer, J. A. and Haugtvedt, C. P. (1987) A reply to Stiff and Boster. *Communication Monographs*, 54, 257–263.

Petty, R. E., Kasmer, J. A., Haugtvedt, C. P. and Cacioppo, J. T. (1987) Source and message factors in persuasion: a reply to Stiff's critique of the Elaboration Likelihood Model. *Communication Monographs*, 54, 233–249.

Petty, R. E., Haugtvedt, C. P. and Smith, S. M. (1995) Elaboration as a determinant of attitude strength: creating attitudes that are persistent, resistant and predictive of behaviour. In: R. E. Petty and J. A. Krosnick (eds), *Attitude strength: antecedents and consequences.* Mahwah, NJ: Erlbaum.

Pfau, M., Van Bockern, S. and Kang, J. G. (1992) Use of inoculation to promote resistance to smoking initiation among adolescents. *Communication Monographs, 59,* 213–230.

Posner, S. F., Baker, L., Heath, A. and Martin, N. G. (1996) Social contact, social attitudes, and twin similarity. *Behavior Genetics, 26,* 123–133.

Potter, J. and Wetherell, M. (1987) *Discourse and social psychology: beyond attitudes and behaviour.* London: Sage.

Prislin, R. and Pool, G. J. (1996) Behavior, consequences, and the self: is all well that ends well? *Personality and Social Psychology Bulletin, 22,* 933–948.

Pryor, J. B. and Merluzzi, T. V. (1985) The role of expertise in processing social interaction scripts. *Journal of Experimental Social Psychology, 21,* 362–379.

Pyszczynski, T., Greenberg, J., Solomon, S., Sideris, J. and Stubbing, M. J. (1993) Emotional expression and the reduction of motivated cognitive bias: evidence from cognitive dissonance and distancing from victims paradigms. *Journal of Personality and Social Psychology, 64,* 177–186.

Roese, N. J. and Jamieson, D. W. (1993) Twenty years of bogus pipeline research: a critical review and meta-analysis. *Psychological Bulletin, 114,* 363–375.

Rogers, C. R. (1980) *A way of being.* Boston: Houghton Mifflin.

Rogers, R. W. (1975) A protection motivation theory of fear appeals and attitude change. *Journal of Psychology, 91,* 93–114.

Rogers, R. W. (1983) Cognitive and physiological processes in fear appeals and attitude change: a revised theory of protection motivation. In: J. Cacioppo and R. Petty (eds), *Social psychophysiology.* New York: Guilford Press.

Rosenberg, M. J. (1960) An analysis of affective-cognitive consistency. In: C. Hovland, and M. Rosenberg (eds), *Attitude organization and change.* New Haven, CT: Yale University Press.

Rubin, A. M. (1994) Media uses and effects: a uses and gratifications perspective. In: J. Bryant and D. Zillmann (eds) (1994), *Media effects: advances in theory and research.* Hillsdale, NJ: Erlbaum.

Sarver, V. T. (1983) Ajzen and Fishbein's 'Theory of Reasoned Action': a critical assessment. *Journal for the Theory of Social Behaviour, 13,* 155–163.

Schachter, S. and Singer, J. (1962) Cognitive, social, and physiological determinants of the emotional state. *Psychological Review*, 69, 379–399.

Shavitt, S. (1989) Operationalizing functional theories of attitudes. In: A. R. Pratkanis, S. J. Brecker and A. G. Greenwald (eds), *Attitude structure and function*. Hillsdale, NJ: Erlbaum.

Shavitt, S. (1990) The role of attitude objects in attitude functions. *Journal of Experimental Social Psychology*, 26, 124–148.

Shepherd, G. J. and O'Keefe, D. J. (1984) Separability of attitudinal and normative influences on behavioural intentions in the Fishbein-Ajzen model. *Journal of Social Psychology*, 122, 287–288.

Sherif, M. and Hovland, C. I. (1961) *Social judgement: assimilation and contrast effects in communication and attitude change*. New Haven, CT: Yale University Press.

Sherif, M., Harvey, L. J., White, B. J., Hood, W. R. and Sherif, C. W. (1961) *The Robbers Cave experiment: inter-group conflict and co-operation*. Middletown, CT: Wesleyan University Press.

Sigall, H. (1997) Ethical considerations in social psychological research: is the bogus pipeline a special case? *Journal of Applied Social Psychology*, 27, 574–581.

Sluckin, W., Colman, A. M. and Hargreaves, D. J. (1980) Liking words as a function of the experienced frequency of their exposure. *British Journal of Psychology*, 71, 163–169.

Smith, B. L., Lasswell, H. D. and Casey, R. D. (1946) *Propaganda, communication and public opinion*. Princeton, NJ: Princeton University Press.

Snyder, M. and DeBono, K. (1989) Understanding the functions of attitudes: lessons from personality and social behaviour. In: A. R. Pratkanis, S. J. Breckler and A. G. Greenwald (eds), *Attitude structure and function*. Hillsdale, NJ: Erlbaum.

Steele, C. M. (1988) The psychology of self-affirmation: sustaining the integrity of the self. In: L. Berkowitz (ed.), *Advances in experimental social psychology, vol. 21*. New York: Academic Press.

Steele, C. M., Southwick, L. L. and Critchlow, B. (1981) Dissonance and alcohol: drinking your troubles away. *Journal of Personality and Social Psychology*, 41, 831–846.

Stiff, J. B. (1986) Cognitive processing of persuasive message cues: a meta-analytic review of the effects of supporting information on attitudes. *Communication Monographs*, 53, 75–89.

REFERENCES

Stiff, J. B. and Boster, F. J. (1987) Cognitive processing: additional thoughts and a reply to Petty, Kasmer, Haugtvedt and Cacioppo. *Communication Monographs, 54,* 250–256.

Stone, D. (1998) Principles and pragmatism in the privatisation of British higher education. *Policy and Politics, 26,* 3, 255–271.

Sutton, S. (1987) Social psychological approaches to understanding addictive behaviours: attitude-behaviour and decision-making models. *British Journal of Addiction, 82,* 355–370.

Terry, D. J. and Hogg, M. A. (2000) *Attitudes, Behaviour and Social Context: The Role of Norms and Group Membership.* Mahwah, NJ: Erlbaum.

Tesser, A. (1993) The importance of heritability in psychological research – the case of attitudes. *Psychological Review, 100,* 129–142.

Tesser, A. (1998) Attitude heritability, attitude change, and physiological responsivity. *Personality and Individual Differences, 24,* 89–96.

Thomas, W. I. and Znaniecki, F. (1918) *The Polish peasant in Europe and America.* Boston: Badger.

Thurstone, L. L. (1931) The measurement of social attitudes. *Journal of Abnormal Social Psychology, 26,* 249–269.

Thurstone, L. L. and Chave, E. J. (1929) *The measurement of attitudes.* Chicago: University of Chicago Press.

Tourangeau, R., Smith, T. W. and Rasinski, K. A. (1997) Motivation to report sensitive behaviours on surveys: evidence from a bogus pipeline experiment. *Journal of Applied Social Psychology, 27,* 209–222.

Valdiserri, R. O., Arena, V. O., Proctor, D. and Bonati, F. A. (1989) The relationship between women's attitudes about condoms and their use: implications for condom promotion campaigns. *American Journal of Public Health, 79,* 499–503.

van Harreveld, F., van der Pligt, J. and de Vries, N. K. (1999) Attitudes towards smoking and the subjective importance of attributes: implications for changing risk benefit ratios. *Swiss Journal of Psychology, 58,* 65–72.

Warr, P. B. (1965) Proximity as a determinant of positive and negative sociometric choice. *British Journal of Social and Clinical Psychology, 4,* 104–109.

Wicker, A. W. (1969) Attitudes versus actions: the relationship of verbal and overt behavioural responses to attitude objects. *Journal of Social Issues, 25,* 41–78.

Witte, K. (1992) Putting the fear back into fear appeals: the extended parallel process model. *Communication Monographs, 59*, 329–349.

Wood, J. V. (1989) Theory and research concerning social comparisons of personal attributes. *Psychological Bulletin, 106*, 231–248.

Wood, W. and Eagly, A. H. (1981) Stages in the analysis of persuasive messages: the role of causal attributions and message comprehension. *Journal of Personality and Social Psychology, 40*, 246–259.

Zajonc, R. B. (1968) Attitudinal effects of mere exposure. *Journal of Personality and Social Psychology Monograph Supplement, 9* (2), 1–27.

Zhang, X., Wang, L., Zhu, X. and Wang, K. (1999) Knowledge, attitude and practice survey on immunization service delivery in Guangxi and Gansu, China. *Social Science and Medicine, 49*, 1125–1127.

Index